HEXPECTATIONS

Breaking the Curse of Unspoken, Unrealistic, and Unmet Expectations

LYNELLE FOLKERT

Published by Redemption Press, PO Box 427, Enumclaw, WA 98022, (360) 226-3488.

Redemption Press is honored to present this title in partnership with the author. The views expressed or implied in this work are those of the author. Redemption Press provides our imprint seal representing design excellence, creative content, and high-quality production.

ISBN 13: 978-1-64645-708-3 (Paperback)
978-1-64645-714-4 (Hard cover)
978-1-64645-732-8 (eBook)

Library of Congress Catalog Card Number: 2024905404

To Brent, who really gets me and still loves me.

CONTENTS

ACKNOWLEDGEMENTS

I WONDER HOW many people read the acknowledgments section. Confession: I have been a skimmer.

Now that I have experienced the agonizing time and intention it takes to pull this off, I'm gonna read others' more often. I will give it my best shot to name those who helped make this book a reality.

I first acknowledge you, the reader. I have lived with this feeling of hexpectations my whole life, and it nearly wrecked me. Discovering this word to name the behavior has helped. If you can shift your mindset about expectations of self and others even a little, my anxious days writing the book were worth it.

Sean, I finally wrote the book. Thank you for being so darn blunt telling me repeatedly how this word needed to be shared so others could free themselves of the curse of falling short.

Kory, you said, "Yeah, this word totally makes sense and should be a four-part teaching series." Ha ha. Who knows, but thanks for believing in me and encouraging me to keep at it.

I couldn't have done it without my beta-read feedback groupies, Sean, Kory, Craig, Rosanne, Kim, Megan, Steve,

Addair, Brian, Renee, Kathlyn, and anyone else I mentioned the concept to or who read parts of it. Your advice and encouragement meant the world to me.

My Celebrate Recovery teammates, open share and forever family accept and challenge me to keep coming back 'cause it works if I work it and it won't if I don't, and I am worth it. Brian, specifically, thanks for the cover and for telling me to use the word sexpectations.

Jeff, thanks for giving me your time, intelligence, and chats, helping me navigate this "book thing" you know so well.

Ross and Athena, thank you for really getting this word and championing me onward. Our zoom calls and your handiwork, Ross, kept me afloat. Mari and the Redemption Press crew are gems for patiently handling a first timer like me.

To the rest of my friends, small group, family, Tuesday morning prayer warriors, Boundaries.me group, PCCI cohorts, and perfect strangers who heard me talk about this word, you know who you are. I am grateful and love you. But if I list everyone, this will get too long, and people like me won't read it.

Brent, Megan, Joel, Ben, Marissa, Sean, and Charlotte, I am truly thankful and humbled as your wife, mom, in-law, and second mom.

Jesus, thank you for saving a wretch like me. Your grace is so amazing.

INTRODUCTION

ROSIE IS STANDING in the checkout line, frustrated. She sees a couple across the aisle. "Look how he loads the groceries for her. She is so lucky. If I had a man who helped me like that, I'd be happy." She looks at Bill thumbing through a magazine beside her. Internally she wishes he would turn and ask, "Anything I can do for you, honey?" Because he doesn't, she seethes with scorn. Sadly, he has no idea what she's thinking.

Ever had one of those moments? You might not be consciously aware of the many unarticulated expectations luring you to think someone should just know or do or be exactly what you want. If you've been alive for more than five minutes, my guess is you have had these thoughts too.

Allow me to rephrase similar expectations that lead to conflict and disconnection by calling them something completely different. They feel like an unseen hook.

Hex·pec·ta·tion (hɛkˌspɛkˈteɪʃən) 1. *v.* to place a harmful illusion on a desired outcome that is not spoken, not based on actual facts, and not able to be met without mutual agreement.

I thought of this word and have let it rummage around in my head for a while now. I experience it and see it in others continuously as a life discovery coach. Unhinging myself from its cursing effects inspired my writing to help you uncover your own unspoken, unrealistic thoughts that leave you with unmet expectations.

EXPLORING HEXPECTATIONS

CHAPTER ONE

THE NEW WORD

People who chase outcome-based happiness are at
the mercy of circumstances beyond their control.
People who live by their values stumble
across happiness often.

—STEVE NORMAN

THE TEXT READS, "Can we talk?" Immediately I sift through our interactions wondering what in the world this could be about. I start getting that creepy-crawly feeling that I did or said something wrong again. Some might say those are code words for "it's serious." Hit the panic button.

If you're anything like me, you have felt significant pressure around the word *expectation*. I have struggled with trying to figure out what other people want from me and working to meet those expectations but have never felt I measured up. Frankly, I've also done this to others, wanting them to act a certain way and becoming frustrated and angry when they didn't act the way I wanted. Why do I keep blaming others for not living up to my expectations instead of examining whether my expectations are the problem? Seemingly unanswerable questions plagued my thoughts: Why don't things work out how I want? How can I make others happy with me? How can I even make myself happy?

Sometimes these thoughts originate from me, and sometimes they come from others. Often these situations are accompanied by a backhanded notion, "It's never enough," which leads me to believe "I'm not enough." Sigh.

From wherever they stem, these beliefs often bloom into destructive resentments and despair. If you've ever felt that weight, this book is for you. If you know someone who labors under the burden of expectations, slip them a copy too.

Right now, I'm sitting at my kitchen counter looking at the large remodeling project we started over a year ago that remains unfinished. I thought that *last* Christmas we would be sitting in the new space, enjoying it together. This was unspoken as an expectation. It also was unrealistic for the scope of the project. When I start feeling uptight and resentful toward my husband for not having it finished yet, I take a mental step back. I remind myself we mutually agreed to work on this project in our spare time with spare funds. It will get done when it gets done. However, my thoughts have copious amounts of hidden expectations that he'll get it done when *I want* it done.

I know life doesn't always go according to plan. Getting uptight about unrealistic expectations only leads to frustration. So, I must be patient and flexible—two words I'm still learning how to incorporate into my DNA.

While writing this book, I got this chest-grabbing panicky feeling, thinking, *I can't do this; it's too hard.* These are silent self-limiting mindsets that suffocate. I hexpect it will be a total waste of time, energy, and resources that keeps me on the roller-coaster ride of starting and stopping continually.

Identifying how these toxic thoughts were poisoning the fruit of my existence was the genesis of the term *hexpectation.* Allow me to restate my definition.

Hex·pec·ta·tion (hɛkˌspɛkˈtéɪʃən) 1. *v.* to place a harmful illusion on a desired outcome that is not spoken, not based on actual facts, and not able to be met without mutual agreement.

This book explores the concept of hexpectations and how they can be understood and changed to help people overcome the curse of disappointment.

I'm still fleshing this word out. What does it actually mean? How can I explain it well enough so people even get it? What if it's a complete flop? The self-doubt and second-guessing are hexhausting!

I don't know you; your beliefs may differ from mine greatly or slightly. Either way, I've allowed my faith in Jesus to anchor my perspective in writing about this subject. You don't have to agree with me to gain some insight into how this concept is affecting your life. I hope this knowledge empowers you to reframe your thoughts about expectations of yourself and others. It may even lead to understanding God a little better along the way.

This book is divided into three sections:

1. Exploring Hexpectations
2. Experiencing Hexpectations
3. Breaking Hexpectations

The first section fleshes out how our desired outcomes, without speaking them out loud, give our expectations little to no ability of being met. How often are the thoughts we play with laced with unrealistic, improbable criteria? What is the fallout when things don't go as you thought they would?

The second section gives examples of how I've seen hexpectations play out in my life and the people around me. I trust you will see yourself in a few of these prime illustrations of where hexpectations happen in our lives.

The third section discusses how to work toward unity in our thoughts, how to speak them confidently and clearly, how to trust that change takes time given intention and consistency, and how to let yourself bask in the grace that accepts outcomes as growth opportunities.

Use this book. Write in it. Dog-ear the pages. Step back from it to investigate how this word is showing up in your life. Are you hexpecting things to happen a certain way and feeling cursed when they don't?

CHAPTER TWO

DEFINING EXPECTATIONS

A master can tell you what he expects of you.
A teacher, though, awakens your own expectations.

—PATRICIA NEAL

LIVING EMOTIONALLY AND spiritually healthy lives requires us to engage correctly with expectations. If values shape our lives, expectations color what we think is reliable.

The Cambridge Dictionary defines *expectation* as "the feeling that good things are going to happen in the future."[1] But that doesn't really cover it, does it? Sometimes our expectations are dreadful—that bad things, unwanted things, or hurtful things are on the horizon. It's kind of a mixed bag.

---

1. Cambridge Dictionary Online, s.v. "expectation (n.)," accessed August 12, 2024, https://dictionary.cambridge.org/dictionary/english/expectation.

Expectations are not the enemy. We all live with routine, recognized, and responsible expectations, which is sensible and necessary for healthy relationships to flourish. How much stock are we placing in what we are expecting? Further, it is important that we discuss what happens when our expectations are rejected.

Routine Expectations

Routine expectations are based on our experience that something will happen repeatedly, such as going to sleep and expecting to wake up. Ecclesiastes 3:1–8 shares many routine expectations of everyday life, starting with, "There is a time for everything, and a season for every activity under the heavens: a time to be born and a time to die, a time to plant and a time to uproot ... a time to weep and a time to laugh, a time to mourn and a time to dance."

Some routines we don't even think about consciously, like breathing. We expect the earth to make a twenty-four-hour rotation with daylight and darkness and to travel around the sun in 365 days. Routine expectations have a nod to the normal. It has happened before, and it most likely will happen again.

As a noun, *routine* is normally understood as a sequence of actions regularly followed; a fixed program. As an adjective, it describes something performed as part of a regular procedure rather than for a special reason.

My husband gets up at the same time every day. He follows a string of activities and rarely deviates. He comes home from work at nearly the same time and nowadays lets me know if he will be late. A routine is something that's not out of the ordinary. We count on people's routines, which makes them predictable and familiar.

Responsible Expectations

Responsible expectations feel attainable by everyone and within reach of all given a practical amount of effort. Recognized expectations are common respectful behaviors such as "don't spit at people" and "don't hit others." These are things we teach our kids. Most everyone wants others to recognize these as normal and acceptable.

I've heard it said that if you're on time you're late, and if you're late, don't bother. *On time* to some means arriving five to ten minutes early. Truly, I recognize the expectation of timeliness, but sometimes I'm late. When I'm labeled as always late by others, they will hexpect me to be late for everything and label me irresponsible. What I'm involved with is a hexpectation. I am cursed before even trying.

Someone once accused me of being an optimistic person in that I expect to be able to complete one more task before I need to be anywhere. It was a kind gesture.

A common scenario: if our boss tells us a promotion is coming and it's communicated clearly, then ideally, we count on it at some point. This is not saying it *will* happen, but given reinforcing information from our boss, we recognize this expectation is reasonable, that we can depend on it.

If you want work done on your house a certain way, there are normally contracts created and signed by all parties involved. What a novel idea—having a mutual agreement to meet expectations.

Certain expectations keep society safe, such as not murdering, stealing, or driving down the wrong side of the road. They are not automatic and require commitment to society at large.

For a marriage to be successful, it takes two people to commit to what they are vowing to do for the other person for life. Merging two different households of upbringing and experiences takes a *lot* of ongoing conversations to discover what you desire with and from the other person. Ideally, this ensures the marriage will not crash on the shores of unmet expectations.

When parents bring home a baby from the hospital, it is expected that they will devote their lives to love and protect that child until it reaches adulthood. As we are all painfully aware, this is not always a fulfilled expectation.

It is a responsible expectation that people work for a living and support themselves and their families the best they can. The Bible tells us, "Whatever you do, work at it with all your heart, as working for the Lord, not for human masters, since you know that you will receive an inheritance from the Lord as a reward. It is the Lord Christ you are serving" (Colossians 3:23–24).

Rejected Expectations

Just because we have recognized, responsible expectations by most people doesn't make them realized. Having expectations is not the problem. When known expectations are rejected, it can create heartache, disconnection, and disaster.

When people reject promptness as a healthy, normal expectation, they leave others feeling as if they don't matter. This leads to resentment and possibly an expectation by others that they're never going to arrive at anything on time.

We recognize red lights are for stopping. What happens when someone is late for a meeting and rejects that seemingly responsible expectation to STOP, hitting the gas pedal instead of the brake? This action could cause them to crash into an unsuspecting mom taking her kids to school because she is living with the normal expectation that green means go and red means stop.

God gave Adam and Eve everything in the garden of Eden except one tree. He asked them to be responsible. They were not content and wandered too close to the forbidden tree that would teach them good and evil. When the serpent instilled doubt about God's words in their minds, they rejected the expectation that God had given them for their own benefit. This choice led to their expulsion from the garden and the introduction of sin and death into the world.

Often, we don't even know we *have* expectations until they go unmet. We truly forget others don't think the same way we do. Sometimes it's hard to accept that there are other ways to do things, see situations, and experience life. We often catch ourselves in the web of unmet expectations because we live on autopilot, assuming others agree with us. Gaining understanding and clarity enhances our ability to get what we expect.

I wonder where you are feeling the sting of rejected expectations from someone. Maybe even yourself. Do others know exactly what you want? Have they agreed to it? Ultimately, reliability is what we are looking for in having expectations. When what we expect isn't what we get, anxiety swoops in and casts its spell on our believing that anyone will come through for us.

CHAPTER THREE

HOW HEXPECTATIONS HAPPEN

You can't heal a wound by saying it's not there.

—SEE JEREMIAH 6:14

THE IDEA OF hexpectations was born one day while catching up with my friend Sara about our roles in life. I shared my discouragement—my exhaustion over feeling let down and letting others down when I don't live up to my and others' expectations.

Sara and her husband were hired to a midsized growing community church. "We were new and had energy and ideas about how to accomplish many things. However, we never seemed to measure up to their hidden expectations, let alone ours. We thought they wanted change and new programs to be instituted. There was this sense we just weren't getting it quite right. They never said it directly, but we could feel it from their cold shoulders."

I nodded. "It's as if they had hexpectations."

Sara jerked her head in my direction. "What did you say?"

I repeated, "Hexpectations."

"That's it," she said. "That's exactly what it felt like. Like we were damned if we did and damned if we didn't."

In Sara's mind, she hoped living in a small American town and ministering to a tight-knit group of people would fulfill a longing for purpose on a deep spiritual level. However, continuously feeling the pressure of not measuring up to the unclear, hidden expectations from the other families in their community left her feeling defeated.

Even as I'm writing this, my grammar program keeps trying to correct me, underlining the word *hexpectations*, saying "not a word." Not yet, but maybe it's gonna be.

A word like *hexpectations* might freak some people out. Rest assured, I'm not suggesting we're witches and wizards riding around on broomsticks and casting spells on people or that we have voodoo dolls in our closets. However, I do believe our thoughts and unspoken words have power. Hexpectations are unspoken, often unrealistic thoughts that trap our thinking.

***

Hex means to curse. It is unseen. These are invisible, silent, unrealistic, or negative thoughts or projections on others or situations causing misery or harm.

An *expectation* is a fixed idea that something will or should happen in a certain way. We might guess, calculate, or predict how that outcome will happen but strongly believe it will.

Thus, a *hexpectation* results when we build a situation up in our hidden, unspoken thoughts and feel miserable when it doesn't get fulfilled. We believe the worst-case scenario and suffer needlessly in silence.

They also happen when we envision specific, possibly even grandiose, outcomes of situations, assuming everyone is on board with what we think should happen. When life doesn't measure up to our scripted play-by-play, disappointment and frustration become constant companions. We walk around with this pin of pain in our brain because this thing did not turn out the way we *thought* it should. We might even blame everyone else instead of seeing how our romanticized ideal corrupts outcomes.

We might even hexpect that a person who has let us down before will continue to do so. We label them with "always" or "never" feeling stuck, unable to shake our negative view of them or their performance.

Conversely, having a grotesquely positive hexpectation of a person that is both an unspoken and unrealistic ideal may leave us feeling uptight or angry when they don't act the way we envisioned.

John A. Johnson, professor at Pennsylvania State, wrote, "For many of us, it is difficult to let go of the idea that *expecting* something to happen will *make* it happen.... If I believe that my expectations alone will bring me what I want, I am using magical thinking [which is a hexpectation] and setting myself up for disappointment."[2]

Hexpectations are tricky. They happen between our ears. We doubt our abilities and fear failure, which prevents us from trying new things. Doom and gloom play in the shadows of our minds, snuffing out hope that anything can turn out for our good. We let perfectionism poison the potential for positive alternate outcomes because we get stuck ruminating over how to manipulate all the parts and pieces.

I would like to bring our unconscious tendencies of thinking into the light. Often, we don't even know we have an expectation until it bumps against someone else with a different one. It then becomes an argument about who is right and wrong versus communicating differences to gain better understanding.

---

2   John A. Johnson, "The Psychology of Expectations," *Psychology Today,* February 17, 2018, https://www. psychologytoday.com/us/blog/cui-bono/201802/the-psychology-expectations.

When we continually predict unrealistic or negative outcomes, our lives become tainted with a deadly feeling of discouragement. The weight of that hidden disappointment happening over and over is suffocating, like a hex.

Our thoughts are unspoken words with the same power to hurt or heal. Left unchecked, our unspoken words can be just as damaging as the ones we utter, because our thoughts are actions in the making. King David beseeched God in the Psalms, "Search me, O God, and know my heart: try me and know my thoughts" (Psalm 139:23 KJV). His son, King Solomon, warned us in Proverbs, "Death and life are in the power of the tongue" (Proverbs 18:21 KJV). The word *hexpectation* is a useful way to name the power of our unspoken, unrealistic thoughts that aren't in line with God's best for our lives or beneficial for those around us.

CHAPTER FOUR

DEFINING HEXPECTATIONS

The more accurately you can name something,
the easier it is to deal with it.

—BRENÉ BROWN

SO, LET'S TALK about how routine, recognized, and responsible expectations become hexpectations. A hexpectation has a backhanded hook to it. It causes pressure in your mind and body and leads you to believe you are in control of the outcome or that the outcome had better measure up to your ideals or those placed on you from the outside.

For our purpose here, there are three kinds of hexpectations that affect us.

Unspoken Hexpectations

Unspoken hexpectations happen when we keep expectations to ourselves but hold others responsible for meeting them. People can't meet expectations they don't know exist. We make the mistake of thinking it takes too much time and effort to clarify everything verbally. It takes far more time to unhinge ourselves from messy relationships and situations if we haven't clarified our objectives.

If you want expectations met, be sure to say them clearly. Renowned researcher and speaker Brené Brown coined the popular phrase "Clear is kind. Unclear is unkind."[3]

When others are involved, I must share my thoughts out loud, asking for verbal agreement and understanding of the expectation. My husband asks me to send him an email regarding requests I have of him so he can put it on his schedule. I used to think this was silly. Can't he just listen better when I ask for something? Having it written helps him transfer it into his schedule. It's kind because it's clearly spoken.

Our son mows the lawns for our rental homes after he finishes his day job. I wanted them mowed before the grass blades sprout and before 8 p.m. so as not to disturb the guests. When I live with hexpectations branding my brain, I just hope or assume he knows what I want. No one can read minds. If something is not said out loud, it's not clear.

---

3   Brené Brown, "Clear Is Kind. Unclear is Unkind," Brené Brown, October 15, 2018, https://brenebrown.com/ articles/2018/10/15/clear-is-kind-unclear-is-unkind/.

I thought, *He's mowed lawns for a company before. I hope he knows what I mean when I say mow them before they get too long.* When an expectation is unspecified or unclear, it will become a hexpectation because of what happens when he doesn't do what I thought he should. I'll be frustrated he didn't measure up to my unspoken ideas, leaving him feeling cursed for even trying.

I typed a contract with our son, outlining what I needed him to do to fulfill the job. I asked him to go over it with me. We discussed anything he didn't understand. We both signed it with a date to witness that he agreed to what I wanted, and I agreed to pay him for the job.

I used to hate confrontation, and opposition scared me, so silence felt easier than voicing what I needed. Why are we so scared to say what we think or need? Is being pissed off or fed up more comfortable than being clear? Having expectations is not the problem; it's how we vocalize them. The goal is to do so with a kind tone, open to discussing the reasonableness of said expectation.

The Bible depicts two sisters in Luke chapter 10 caught in one of these silent fiascos. Martha opened her home for Jesus and his disciples to rest from their travels. Surely her sister would help serve this troop hanging out in their home. Nope. Sister Mary took a seat listening to the Rabbi's powerful teachings while Martha got distracted by all the preparations that had to be made. Picture Martha huffing and puffing slamming pots on the floor, mixing loudly, thinking resentful thoughts about her sister being lazy and unhelpful.

Fed up with doing it all by herself, she marched into the room hexpecting Jesus to chastise Mary into helping her with the fanfare. I imagine his tone was soft and caring when he said "Martha, Martha, you are worried and upset about many things, but few things are needed.... Mary has chosen what is better, and it will not be taken away from her [by you obsessing over it]" (Luke 10:41–42). He probably wanted Martha to come take a seat and relax in His presence, learning how to feel at peace versus pressured.

Unrealistic Hexpectations

We have unrealistic hexpectations when we feel discomfort as our reality falls short of our expectations. My friend Shirley says, "We know if an expectation is set too high when it can't be met consistently ... or at all." It doesn't negate setting high goals, but they need to be paired with healthy reality.

Looking up the word *unrealistic* brought two other hex-like words: *romantic* and *perfectionistic*. Romance is often unrealistic. Hmm. That's interesting. Many think the scenes they watch on the screen or read in a book are romantic, setting their imperfect relationships up with hexpectations. Relationships are cursed continually when held to unreasonable standards of relating to each other. If you want someone to act out what you see on the screen or in a book, I guarantee they will feel cursed by you hexpecting they pretend for you. After all, a book is fantasy, and a movie or TV show is acting. It's not real. It may be fun for a moment, but imitation isn't authentic.

We also need to accept that perfection isn't possible. *Perfect* means flawless, unblemished. Nothing and no one can be perfect on this side of heaven. "All have sinned and fall short of the glory of God" (Romans 3:23). I fall short. My husband falls short. My house falls short. Everything has the characteristics of falling short. That should come as a relief. Sadly, many strive for unattainable perfection because they aren't content to accept this fact. They keep searching for perfection in their job, things, or people to fill a void that's incapable of being filled with anything other than the gift of grace through a surrendered relationship with Jesus Christ.

Often, we marry expecting our partner to fulfill all our emotional, physical, and social needs. No one person can be everything to another person. Hexpecting our partner to be everything to us is unrealistic and can lead to sadness and scorn.

Additionally, we can't expect to change our partner after we get married. If we're not happy with aspects of our partner, talk openly about these issues, or we're gonna choke on the words "for better or worse, in sickness and in health." Trying to change our partner is manipulative and can damage the relationship.

Then there are times when our expectations are laced with entitlement. If I watch someone's child for a day when their babysitter cancels, assuming they will return the same kindness is unrealistic. It doesn't mean my service was unappreciated; it just means it didn't come with the hexpectation of paybacks. It was never discussed or agreed upon, which are two key ingredients to ensure meeting an expectation.

We may have unrealistic expectations of a friendship, coworker, boss, pastor, teacher, sister, or parent.

To check if you have unrealistic hexpectations, observe how you respond or react when things don't go as planned. I used to go from zero to one hundred in a flash. My personal reactor factor has diminished significantly. I've realized I'm not in control of as much as I thought. I can hope for specific outcomes without letting my mental expectations be so limiting that I cannot accept any other result. I expect to do my best. That is in my control. What I accept as my best is in proportion to the effort I put forth.

I haven't given up having hopes and dreams, but those are now communicated and paired with a healthy dose of accepting that the future is not often controllable. I can plan, prepare, and then walk forward with expectancy that whatever happens will be an experience I get to learn something from.

Unmet Hexpectations

Unmet hexpectations cause pain. Some say William Shakespeare said, "Expectation is the root of all heartache."[4] It is true—unmet expectations feel miserable, but expectations don't have to end in pain. So often, we have hexperience where something went wrong before, and we get sucked into thinking it will continue to go wrong again. Someone let us down and didn't come through, so we hexpect they'll do it again or someone else will.

I trust you're reading this book because you want to learn how to stop having hexpectations. You want to stop just hoping for the best and expecting the worst. Acting this way will cause you to live life defensively in a perpetual state of thinking something will always go wrong. Believing that things will never work out for you and that life will be awful is a really lousy way to live. I understand it though. Self-protection is instinctual. We guard ourselves from others to avoid repeated disappointment. I have built some pretty thick walls against people who have hurt me or

---

4   Duane Morin, "Expectation Is the Root of All Heartache," Shakespeare Geek, August 25, 2010, https://www.shakespearegeek.com/2010/08/expectation-is-the-root-of-all-heartache.html.

repeatedly said things I have trouble getting beyond. There is certainly a place for self-protection. This is not to dispel the appropriateness of self-agency. I'm simply wanting us to see how we prescript many current, or future, scenarios with negative predictions based on past experience.

Scripture has taught me I have a Father in heaven with a Spirit I've invited to live within me who is my Strength, my Rock, my Fortress, my Deliverer. It is God, in whom I take refuge and let be my shield, my stronghold (Psalm 18:1–2). I lean into the knowledge that I can protect myself logically and emotionally while simultaneously allowing for vulnerability. I can look at the past to inform my present. However, it doesn't need to dictate my reactions. I can pause and assess the situation and respond with confidence in what I need or know at the moment.

In life coach training, I learned a technique called the "meta view," or pulling up to the thirty-thousand-foot outlook over a situation with clients. It helps to get distance above themselves and look down, back, ahead, and around to discover what other possibilities exist to propel them forward in their desired goals and relationships. A top view is better, where we plan for the best but prepare for anything. It might come off as we hope.

CHAPTER FIVE

DESCRIBING HEXPECTATIONS

The truth is that our finest moments
are most likely to occur when we are feeling
deeply uncomfortable, unhappy, or unfulfilled.
For it is only in such moments, propelled by our
discomfort that we are likely to step out of our ruts
and start searching for different ways
or truer answers.

—M. SCOTT PECK

THIS WORD IS not in any dictionary. It's a work in progress. I'm inviting you to notice the motives, feelings, and thoughts fueling your expectations and those others may have of you. How does it feel when things don't go the way you want?

The following are a few situations where I describe what could be classified as hexpectations. Several of these could fall into both the unspoken and unrealistic camps but separating them seemed to help highlight how it happens.

Unspoken and Unrealistic Hexpectations of Self

Self-doubting, fearing failure, and perfectionism are hexpectations limiting our potential for positive experiences. Adverse assumptions insert what we think to be true without any reinforcing evidence. Lacking clarity in conversations and expectations of outcomes wanted often shows up in our disappointments.

My friends go on dates thinking they need to hide their real opinions and feelings. They believe their struggles or differences are best left masked so the other person can fall in love with their ideal self as opposed to their true self. What do you think happens when they act like someone they aren't to gain something that's not real? They grow exhausted from pretending and fall apart when real cracks show up in their armor under pressure.

I'm writing with the holidays approaching, and the tension of tradition is looming. How often am I held hostage to the must-dos to make room for the gotta-haves? There are gifts to buy and wrap, cookies to bake and eat, and parties to attend and host. We have neighbors to compete with decorations, friends to impress with our outfits, and photos to post of our picture-perfect families. We place such a load on ourselves to make sure the festivities are "successful." I often feel cursed if I get the wrong gift or don't give the correct response to a gift someone gave.

Thinking I must always be positive and uplifting for everyone so that I never have a negative moment is hexhausting. I'm human. But I certainly struggled with wanting to be superhuman. I thought it was up to me to feed, protect, rescue, encourage, teach, train, enlighten, etc. our kids for their lives to be flawless. It was an unrealistic amount of pressure I held over myself.

Hexpectations also materialize when we always think the worst. I got a call this morning from the doctor's office. The radiologist wants me back to do more scans. Thinking *It's going to be awful; I probably have cancer* robs me of peace between now and the not-yet.

The way I think about myself is often complicated. My thoughts affect how I communicate verbally or nonverbally. I still can get hijacked by the internal pressure to perform. The conversations between my ears before I engage my tongue may be warm and kind, but they can also be sarcastic and rude. They determine the framework from which I act.

Imagine if our thoughts were in a visual bubble over our heads for everyone to see. That is either funny or scary depending on the narrative.

An ancient scribe once penned, "For as he thinks in his heart, so is he" (Proverbs 23:7 NKJV).

I have lived with an anxious vise grip over my performance in everything. I *had* to do it perfectly. I *needed* people to like me. I *wanted* to do things well enough that nobody would be mad or criticize me. Frankly, I wanted everyone else to do the same. I felt like Charlie Brown's friend Pigpen, who had a cloud of dirt that followed him everywhere. Likewise, I had an aura of intensity that just hung around me. I am certain people felt it; I just did not see how it was affecting those around me yet.

Unspoken and Unrealistic Hexpectations of Others

If you are thinking "I hope they ..." (fill in the blank) and you're not OK with whatever the result will be, you're placing a hexpectation on others. Why not just tell somebody what you want and gain their mutual understanding and agreement instead? This could prevent a fiasco when it doesn't turn out how you wanted but never spoke up.

Unfortunately, in some cases, others may be unwilling or unable to come to a mutual agreement. In these cases, decide if there are any expectations you can lower without creating resentment, set clear boundaries about what you will or won't be able to do in this situation, and find professional help if you are able.

My friend, who is a caffeine junky, sets the coffee to start brewing at 6:30 a.m. Surely her husband will smell the brewed coffee and think of bringing it to her as she finishes her shower. She doesn't ask and gain his agreement. She *hopes* he will do it for her. When he doesn't, she sputters to herself, "He doesn't care about my need for coffee to face my day happily." She treats him coldly for not fulfilling her hexpectation of delivering said coffee. He's been hexed for not fulfilling her hidden expectation.

You have a favorite actor or celebrity or person you've seen from a distance. Maybe it's your pastor. You've seen their movies or read their books or listened to them teach. You meet them in public expecting them to be what you have envisioned, only to hear them cuss or act rudely or not how you had them set up in your mind to be. You then recreate a negative opinion of them based on the brief interaction that didn't align with your hexpectation. Their humanness is cursed in your mind.

If a husband does the dishes because in his mind he is doing a favor and the result will be he gets sex but his partner doesn't follow through on his hexpectation, he may resort to aggressive or passive-aggressive behaviors to make her feel bad she didn't take the hint.

Another way hexpectations happen is thinking someone owes you. While I was out of town recently, a prescription was ready for me at the pharmacy. My husband, Brent, and I both get the notifications. I expected him to pick it up since I was out of town. Later, my phone pinged revealing Brent hadn't picked up the script yet, and my brain was off to the races: *Is it so hard for him to just do one thing for me? His head is always on his stuff to do. I have things on my mind too: I have a job, school, our kids' schedules, house projects, not to mention the fundraiser, concert to attend, and dinner plans when I get home. Geez!*

I prepared to fire off a nasty text, then it dawned on me. I'm writing a book about hexpectations. In my head, I expected Brent to do what I wanted because of all I do for him and cursed him when he didn't, convincing myself he just did not care and he was blowing me off. Reality revealed I hadn't verbally conferred with him, and he could not verbally agree to it on his timetable.

I was relieved Brent hadn't heard my thoughts and that my text wasn't sent. But does it matter? Scripture says, "For the mouth speaks what the heart is full of" (Matthew 12:34). Although I had merely thought, not spoken, my frustration, what ran through my mind reflected my heart, and it wasn't kind.

A dangerous hexpectation is thinking of all the ways you must change somebody before the relationship gets more serious. People fall in love with the potential of someone, not always with who they exactly are. Worse is when you think you can change them after saying "I do."

I grew up watching *Bewitched*, a sixties sitcom in which Samantha, a good witch, marries a mortal named Darrin. He doesn't know she can make things appear and disappear with the wiggle of her nose.

In one episode, Darrin is sleeping on the couch, and Samantha's mother, Endora, pops in and questions why Samantha would marry someone so ordinary and drab. Samantha swears she loves him as he is, and his appearance is perfectly fine. But then she wonders what would happen if she did change his hair or give him a mustache or alter his nose. With a little tweak here and there, she changes his entire look. When he wakes suddenly and sees his reflection in the mirror, he is astonished and asks his wife why she wants to change him. She tries to explain that she and her mother were just having fun. But the damage is done. He feels demoralized and grows doubtful about his attractiveness. He feels hexed by her expectations that he should look different from the man she married.[5]

As a young girl, I thought of all the things I could do if only I had that nose-twitching ability to alter life. This power would be useful if I could make people and things always turn out how I wanted. I got sucked into living based on the perceptions and lies in my head and not in the reality of my circumstances.

---

5   *Bewitched*, season 1, episode 33, "A Change of Face," created by Sol Saks, Screen Gems/Columbia, aired May 13, 1965.

Unspoken and Unrealistic Hexpectations We Feel from Others

When others place unseen, unknown expectations on us for not feeding their hidden need for control, affirmation, or acknowledgment, they place relationships in jeopardy. When somebody is expecting us to feel sorry for them, it feels like a curse when we don't come to their rescue. Their demeanor toward us is often cold and distant.

It's a form of silent manipulation when someone is hoping you see they are having a bad day and hexpecting you to come and offer help for their self-indulgence. They never ask for it directly. It is implied. It may be a boss, coworker, parent, spouse, or child. It is likely they don't know consciously they are treating you poorly for not catering to their whims. But you can feel it.

Some people search for the perfect gift, expecting you to be ecstatic and deeply appreciative upon discovery. However, they can often act perturbed or dismissive when the response they were looking for falls short of their hopes.

Doing favors for others is another way a hexpectation can be placed. They did something for you, so they expect someday you will do something for them. It's called paybacks. However, unless that favor was discussed openly and agreed upon, there should be no silent hexpectation of you. They are passive-aggressively waiting for you to acknowledge you owe them.

What if you go to lunch with someone, and as a kind gesture for their momentary lack of funds, you pick up the tab? Then every time you go out afterward, there's this hidden expectation that you will do so again and again. Nobody wants to set the record straight that it was a one-time gift, not an ongoing feeding frenzy. There's a thin line between gratitude and entitlement. A hexpectation emerges when we expect unlimited access to others' resources.

Hexpectations from others occur when they hold us at arm's length, acting cold and withdrawn because we didn't get it right by their standards. It's a mental tug-of-war figuring out people's unspoken expectations of us. I felt this at a party when the host was distant toward me throughout the evening. I kept trying to start a conversation, clean up, compliment her on the decorations and food. But the air hung heavy between us. Was she mad at me? Did I forget something? I wondered what she wasn't saying she expected of me.

Relationships become contaminated in many ways when critical or bombastic conversations happen between our ears. When people let us down, it hurts. When life doesn't go the way we want, we're disappointed. I'm not saying we ignore or dismiss our emotions. Instead, I suggest we feel the emotion while managing how it affects our thoughts and actions.

CHAPTER SIX

HEXPECTATIONS AND FAITH

Trusting God enough to guide us down the
best pathway of our life requires us to first
surrender our life to Him.

—HEATHER BIXLER

YOU MAY HAVE no belief in God or are angry or confused about
what you think He is like. However, I don't want you to miss
out on what I'm discovering about His goodness and living
with His amazing grace. I say this to admit it's complicated,
but maybe it can become clearer.

My Hexpectation of the Christian Life

I thought all my problems would be washed away when
I became a Christian. After all, I was surrendering my life to
an all-knowing, all-powerful God. He could just make all my
addictions and mental and physical confusion go away with

the snap of His finger. Couldn't He? I hexpected God to clean up my dirty little habits the instant I invited Him in. My choices had continual consequences, none of which were God's fault but my own. It takes consistency over time to trust that change can happen, and it has for me.

A lady stopped at my house yesterday hoping I would buy the books she was selling. We started talking, and she shared that her friend had just died on Mother's Day. She had prayed and prayed for her to improve, and she did not. "Why didn't God heal her? I must not have had enough faith." Sadly, many people are trapped by this thinking. I even saw a coffee mug recently that reads, "Faith is not believing that God can, it's knowing He will." Sounds like a gross misrepresentation of faith—faith in a God who will do our bidding, no matter what it is.

Prayer can be a form of hexpecting God to deliver on our requests. Prayer is often a misunderstood expectation. Billy Graham wrote, "Prayer is spiritual communication between man and God, a two-way relationship in which man should not only talk to God but also listen to Him. Prayer to God is like a child's conversation with his father. It is natural for a child to ask his father for the things he needs."[6]

---

6   "What Is Prayer?" Billy Graham Evangelistic Association, June 1, 2004, https://billygraham.org/answer/what-is-prayer/.

We pray asking for our daily bread and expecting it will come. We ask, in Jesus's name, for complete healing of our loved one. But when they die, we are left with an empty bed, cursing God for not coming through how we wanted. I believe this is exactly why many people fall away from their faith. They curse God for not giving them what they hexpected He should.

If I pray for something to happen, isn't this the same as having an expectation it will? Isn't receiving all about believing, and isn't believing called faith? What is faith for if not to believe what I want is what I will get?

My personal faith journey resembles climbing Mount Everest, including a lot of times when I couldn't breathe. From a young age, I believed nobody really loved me; they just put up with me. My mind raced continuously, and my mouth definitely tried to keep up. I was a very talkative kid. I wondered if anyone could see the gloom lurking inside me but certainly worked hard at hiding it.

In my teens, I went on a hiking trip and lost a few pounds. Something clicked inside my head, and the continual counting of every calorie helped me escape this feeling of dread that loomed in my soul. I used food restriction, binging, purging, pills, and physical exertion to control the caloric input and output. It was easier to focus on this one thing than the million other things that scared me to death. Life was harder than I expected it to be. I was trying to please everyone at my expense, and the negative mental groove was deep and wide. For years, it got deeper and wider until the lies backed me into a corner, and I saw no way out except to believe everyone would be better off if I were dead.

Crisis

I acted on that lie one night after I broke up with my boyfriend. I overdosed on prescription pills. I woke up in an intensive care unit with a Christian nurse caring for me. After I got out of an inpatient mental facility, she continued to meet with me, listening to my struggles and asking good questions. She believed in me until I could believe in myself. I attended weekly counseling, sometimes up to four times a week. I read powerful, life-giving, encouraging books. I journaled my thoughts, trying to make sense of the way I'd always been but was begging someone to show me how to change it.

I wanted this recovery thing to be quick and easy. I sought a God I didn't know with bargaining prayers: "Lord, if you heal me, I'll do such and such forever." I viewed God as a Santa Claus. Wasn't it His job to give me what I desired? When my prayers weren't answered the way I hoped or as quickly as I wanted, I cursed God. I thought He was mean, uncaring, and withholding. Were these hexpectations of God?

Six months after my overdose, I was visiting some friends in Peoria, Illinois, who were Christians. I was desperately seeking someone or something that could answer my questions and help me see purpose to living. We attended church, and I heard the pastor say there is a God who loves me, who desperately wants me to know Him and trust Him with my life. He invited anyone who wanted to accept this spoken truth personally to come down front. On my knees in reverent submissive hope, I placed my faith in Jesus Christ.

Once I surrendered to Christ's care and control, I memorized a lot of Scripture telling me, "Do not conform to the pattern of this world, but be transformed by the renewing of your mind" (Romans 12:2). Philippians 4:7–8 told me to fill my mind with and meditate on "things true, noble, reputable, authentic, compelling, gracious—the best, not the worst; the beautiful, not the ugly; things to praise, not things to curse" (MSG). I started using Scripture as a weapon against the lies and voices that said to hurt myself and numb out. I began recognizing my emotions and dealing with them instead of stuffing or starving them.

Transformation

I attended Bible college soon after this life-changing decision of surrender. As a Bible student, I was suffering from a compulsive eating disorder and other related behaviors: self-harm, depression, comparing, suicidal ideation. I was a mess, and it all stemmed from what I had allowed into my head.

I remember where I was sitting when Dr. Joe Aldrich, president of Multnomah University, said, "Our presently dominating thoughts control our actions, which impacts our life experience." When my outlook was depressing, I needed to stop letting the cursed one, Satan, fill my mind with doubt, deception, and despair, which are hexpectations. I started allowing the God of hope to fill me with all joy and peace as I trusted in Him so that I would overflow with hope by the power of the Holy Spirit as instructed by Paul in Romans 15:13.

Hebrews 11:1 says, "Now faith is being sure of things hoped for and certain of things not seen." I wrestled with this verse. I decided to research what each word meant.

"Faith" means conviction, belief, reliance.

"Sure" means to be certain, assured, convinced.

"Things hoped for" means craved, desired, wanted.

"Certain" means unwavering, absolute, undoubtful.

"Things not seen" means concealed, invisible, imperceptible.

This was transforming. I realized that desiring or being hopeful for things to turn out how I wanted wasn't the problem. It was learning to let go of the outcomes. Though I couldn't see God, I began trusting He was for me, loved me, and would allow situations in my life for my growth, not to hurt me.

This is an example of misplaced hope in a specific outcome. When the Jewish people saw Jesus riding through the streets of Jerusalem, they shouted, "Hosanna! Blessed is he who comes in the name of the Lord! Blessed is the King of Israel!" (John 12:13). They hexpected Jesus was going to right the wrongs and release them from the shackles of Roman rule. When He didn't do what they thought He should, a week later they were screaming "Take him away! Take him away! Crucify him!" (John 19:15). How often do we hexpect life and God to be the way we want, and when He doesn't show up how we thought He should, we lose hope or reject faith altogether.

Recently, I came across this excellent article that describes the tension well.

> Expectancy ... is having expectations but without definitions and without a timeline or demand of them being filled. It's a perspective switch where we take all our own plans and set them at the foot of the cross. This means we take our hopes and dreams, hold them openhandedly, and choose to live with expectancy for what our Loving Father will do with them....
>
> Having a spirit of expectancy also creates space for the Lord to move, it creates space for

miracles to happen, and it creates space for us to co-create with Him. This means we can be active participants in seeing His will fulfilled in our lives as well as His Kingdom because we continually make the conscious choice to surrender our own demands.... After all, He is the one who knows us best.... When we are able to set aside expectations, we begin to train our hearts and minds to expect God to work His will in our lives instead of forcing ours into reality.

Continually seeking His will with expectancy allows us to notice how He's guiding and directing us. If we can give Him control and trust that He knows what He's doing, it relieves the stress, the fear, and the worry about tomorrow. It can even help heal and relieve the hurts of the past because we know He'll redeem them for good if we let Him.[7]

Daily I share with God about what I need, want, and wish for and leave it in His hands. I trust He hears my prayers. I believe He loves me and will walk and talk with me along life's narrow way. I am an ambassador here

---

7   Jen Ward, "Expectations vs. Expectancy," YWAM Asheville, April 22, 2020, https://ywamasheville.org/ywam-asheville-blog/expectations-vs-expectancy. Used with permission.

on earth living out the good God has created me to do as Ephesians 2:10 tells me to. This doesn't mean everything will be good. It allows me to see that life *is* good because everything I go through has been and is being used to comfort others in their troubles in ways I, too, have been comforted in my life (see 2 Corinthians 1:3–5).

God can't change what you won't hand over to Him. "Don't fret or worry. Instead of worrying, pray. Let petitions and praises shape your worries into prayers, letting God know your concerns. Before you know it, a sense of God's wholeness, everything coming together for good, will come and settle you down. It's wonderful what happens when Christ displaces worry at the center of your life" (Philippians 4:6–7 MSG).

Instead of swinging from side to side between despair and nail-biting hope, I'm learning the art of living calm and composed despite not knowing outcomes. Ruth Haley Barton is the author of several books and resources on the spiritual life. She writes, "The prayer of indifference expresses the fact that we have come to a place where we want God's will—nothing more, nothing less, nothing else.... It is a state of wide openness to God."[8]

---

8   Ruth Haley Barton, "Advent 4: Mary and the Prayer of Indifference," Transforming Center, December 18, 2011, https://transformingcenter.org/2011/12/advent-4-mary-and-the-prayer-of-indifference/.

Deuteronomy chapter 30, verses 19–20, talks about how God set before me a new way to think, to live. He set before me life and death, blessings and curses. "Now choose life so that you and your children may live and that you may love the LORD Your God, listen to his voice, and hold fast to him. For the LORD is your life." Believing that God will sustain me through any conversation, situation, or issue coming my way in the future helps me stand confident.

EXPERIENCING HEXPECTATIONS

CHAPTER SEVEN

HEXING OURSELVES— SELF-SABOTAGE

Our greatest weakness lies in giving up.
The most certain way to succeed is always to try
just one more time.

—THOMAS EDISON

OVERCOMING OUR HEXPECTATIONS is easier said than done.
It starts with awareness. If I don't know I'm doing something,
I can't change it. Once I can see it, I can address it with new
narratives and break away from not speaking up or having
unrealistic expectations that go unmet. I've been working at
it a long time and will keep addressing it all my life.

I've developed a strategy for working through my
natural reactions to certain situations, I call them *hex hacks*.
I've included questions at the end of each section to help you
refocus and rewrite the script in your head or way of doing
something that is free of the constricted mindset that describes
hexpectations.

The Essence of Self-Sabotage

These hexpectations are focused on self-limiting mindsets that may or may not affect others with whom we are in relationship, but they definitely are self-sabotaging. Self-sabotage is people doing, or not doing, things that block their success or prevent them from accomplishing their goals. It can happen consciously or unconsciously. Self-sabotaging behaviors can affect our personal and professional success as well as our mental health.

The Actions of Self-Sabotage

Failure

The difference between being let down and staying down comes when we embrace failure as normal. The hexpectation loop says we are failures and cursed from ever getting anything right. Failure is not a state of being. It's somewhat of a measurement. It may be between complete success and not meeting the goal, but feeling cursed as a failure is not helpful, only hurtful.

Failure is feedback. What is feedback? When you stand too close to a loudspeaker holding a microphone, a gross screeching sound can happen. This means the microphone and loudspeaker are rapidly feeding each other more and more signals until the system overloads. Necessary adjustments on the mixer board must happen to change the sounds.

How often have I tried the same thing again and again with more and more effort hexpecting different results? Sounds like the definition of insanity. But it's so true! In recovery we say, "If nothing changes, nothing changes." We beat ourselves up for "failing" at something but go right back at it with more gusto instead of pulling back to see it from a different perspective.

On her way to becoming a nurse, Rose struggled to pass anatomy. After she failed the first time, she felt like there was no way she could pass; however, she wanted to continue her studies. Rose was petrified she was going to fail again. Turns out, she didn't pass the second time either. Can you sense the "doomed to fail" dread she must have harbored?

Down went her confidence, and she was in a slump of shame. She began seeing a counselor to sort through the negative narratives she was hexperiencing that were making her ineffective in moving ahead with any classes at all. She felt like every time she took any class, she was going to fail and her dreams of becoming a nurse would forever exist outside her grasp. Her counselor encouraged her to reframe that failure as feedback.

Rose took the information learned with her counselor. She got curious. What did she learn from these two failed classes? How could she do things differently? It took stepping back and being patient with the process of discovering new options for breaking the curse of fear. Second Timothy 1:7

(NLT) says, "For God has not given us a spirit of timidity [fear], but of power, love, and self-discipline."

She did not jinx herself with the narrative "I'm doomed to fail." She didn't curse herself saying she *had* to have an A in the class or that she needed 100 percent on everything or it wasn't good enough. She owned her results by saying "I failed to apply myself in the best way to help me pass the first two times." Period. She prepared differently and applied the study habits explained to her, which propelled her positively toward a better outcome.

Guess what? She passed with flying colors the third time through. She has since not needed to repeat a class, and her nursing degree is in hand. "I sought the LORD, and he answered me; he delivered me from all my fears. Those who look to him are radiant; their faces are never covered with shame" (Psalm 34:4–5).

Fearing failure robs people of much-needed energy to put toward positive outcomes. Some of us have hindered our own success at something because we get hijacked thinking about every way it could go wrong or fail. None of us wakes up and says, "Gee, I think I'm going to try to fail at everything I set out to do today." There's wisdom in looking at situations and decisions from differing angles, trying to lower the probability of things going wrong. We all have felt the tension between what we want to happen and what actually does happen. But the matrix of fear needs to be smashed.

A question I ask myself often now is, What's the worst thing that can happen, and who cares if it does? We don't need to fear what others think of us or bash ourselves either. Trying new things shows an acceptance of what is possible.

Yvon Chouinard states, "When everything goes wrong—that's when the adventure starts."[9] When we fear failure, we might not learn the lessons we need to learn. Famous rally car driver Ken Block said, "Sometimes you win a lot more in a failure than you ever could in a win."[10]

Fearing failure prevents us from believing in the possible. God knows our thoughts, and when fear creeps into the corners of our minds, we can remember He is with us. He is for us, and failure isn't final. It's feedback.

The Old Testament prophet Isaiah lived during the Babylonian overthrow of Israel. He warned the people to turn from their wicked ways and follow after God's righteousness despite their circumstances. He assured the people in Isaiah 41:10, "Do not fear, for I am with you; do not be dismayed, for I am your God. I will strengthen

---

9   Yvon Chouinard, quoted in Amber Ooley, "15 Quotes to Inspire Small Business Owners from Yvon Chouinard," LogoMaker, March 11, 2013, https://www.logomaker.com/blog/15-quotes-to-inspire-small-business-owners-from-yvon-chouinard/.

10   Ken Block, quoted in "Ken Block 1967–2023," It's All about the Build, https://www.allaboutthebuild.com/blog/2023/1/ken-block.

you and help you; I will uphold you with my righteous right hand."

Breaking Free from Fear of Failure

Example: I'm not going to try online dating; it will never work out, and I'll feel like a failure.

New Approach: I'm going to try online dating for one year. I will meet people I don't like and who don't like me. This is normal. There's potential that I could meet some great people in the process. I won't know if I don't try.

Hex Hack:

What are you afraid to try at this point in your life?

When fear of failure says don't even try, what new narrative can you try moving forward?

What could you do this week that pushes the fear factor away from you?

Self-Doubt

Poet Suzy Kassem wrote, "Doubt kills more dreams than failure ever will."[11] It's one of Satan's best tactics. He used it on Eve when he asked her in the garden, "Did God really say 'You must not eat from any tree in the garden'?"

---

11   Suzy Kassem, quoted in "Suzy Kassem > Quotes > Quotable Quote," Goodreads, https://www.goodreads. com/quotes/1324440-doubt-kills-more-dreams-than-failure-ever-will.

(Genesis 3:1). Notice he didn't use a statement about what God said. He got her to second-guess what she had already heard. Clever.

Sometimes I find myself stuck in a mental menagerie, doubting my ability to say the right thing. Second-guessing how a call went or an interaction with someone is still a land mine I step on all too often. *Was that question loaded? Did they really mean this when they asked that? Maybe I should have gotten her another gift; what if she doesn't like this one?* These merry-go-round-and-rounds freeze my thoughts, or the doubt just nags in my ear about whether I am capable. It's a curse on my potential.

Last summer, I was on my way to meet with a group of people I viewed as powerfully important. I imagined no one would approach me to converse because of a core lie that says, "Nobody really likes me; they just put up with me." It's a self-fulfilling curse I have allowed to run amok, especially when entering such situations. From that perspective, why would they talk to me? I was setting myself up for a letdown even before I arrived.

I pulled into the parking lot and had a talk with the girl in the mirror. "Lynelle," I said, "you have every right to be here. You were asked to come and experience some worship, teaching, and lunch. What would happen if you went into the meeting thankful for the invitation to learn something new about someone or a situation? Keep it simple."

I stepped out of my car with a changed attitude. I walked in with an open heart and mind to the possibilities. I released any hexpectations that I needed to be acknowledged or talked to or served. I was centered and ready to start a conversation and content if I did not.

It was worshipful. Chris Brown, the pastor of the Well Church in Columbia, Tennessee, shared his journey writing the book *Restored*. It describes his feeling of living an imposter life working for big-name churches and organizations until someone confronted him about what was really going on behind the years of his journey. It's a great story of persevering through personal insecurities while having incredible hope in a God who restores.

When I pitched the idea of this book, he responded, "Yep, I can see how I do this to myself all the time. Great idea. Write the book." I tried not to jinx myself with any comparisons, because I think his book is really great, and my natural inclination is to say, "My book will suck." I started and stopped writing this book several times over the year. To meet me, you might think I am a self-assured middle-aged woman because I'm extroverted, quite friendly, and not afraid to speak my mind. However, I overthink a lot of decisions and details in my life, wondering if I'll ever get it all right. I have experienced some real breakthroughs in this area, but I'm a work in progress.

William Shakespeare once wrote, "Our doubts are traitors and make us lose the good we oft might win, by fearing to attempt."[12] Basically, that means doubt makes us quit. In its simplest form, self-doubt is having a lack of confidence. It's experiencing feelings of uncertainty about one or more aspects of ourselves. Even the most successful business owners or athletes or actors have issues with some self-doubt. Possessing a healthy measure keeps us from making arrogant, reckless decisions about our lives or those in our care. Everyone questions their ability to carry out challenging tasks. It's normal to wonder if you have the chutzpah to accomplish something.

Using a healthy measure of wisdom and courage keeps us balanced. We diminish self-doubt when we step into opportunities for the sheer experience of it without negative judgment or second-guessing. Let's not cave into the nagging inner critic who says we can't. The humble apostle Paul, who was flogged, shipwrecked, imprisoned, and more said, "I can do everything through Christ, who gives me strength" (Philippians 4:13 NLT).

Breaking Free from Self-doubt

Example: I can't apply for that new job. I don't have what it takes.

---

12   William Shakespeare, *Measure for Measure*, ed. Jonathan Crewe (New York: Penguin, 2000), act 1, scene 4, line 79.

New Approach: I'm going to investigate what it will take and step into this new opportunity. I might learn something helpful to better myself.

Hex Hack:

What invasive, doubting thoughts are caught on repeat in your mind?

What *are* some things you have accomplished in your life?

When you hear the self-doubt dialogue whispering in your ear, say five things you know you *can* do.

Worry—Pessimism

Continually making dismal predictions is crippling. This despairing hexpectation showed up when I became engaged. I worried we wouldn't make it to five years of marriage before we got sick of each other and wanted out. We'd fight all the time, and I'd feel trapped. The color was fading from the wedding photo we hadn't even taken yet. I often looked ahead at life with gray and choppy action like the first motion pictures. So fatalistic. Ever felt like that before?

Continually making dismal predictions is crippling with this backhanded curse before we begin: "I'm going to try online dating, but there's nobody out there I'll like." "I'll try that new recipe, but it probably won't turn out." "I'm going to apply for that job, but I probably won't get it." "I want to talk to him, but it will likely end in a fight again."

I struggle with obsessive thinking and anxiety. Recently I made a large purchase. My mind went into overdrive on all the things that could go wrong in the future as a result. I wondered if any studies had been conducted about how many of our unrealistic predictions come true. I was grateful to read a study that said, "Participants with GAD [generalized anxiety disorder] recorded worries when prompted for 10 days, reviewed them online nightly, and tracked their worry outcomes across 30 days.... Primary results revealed that 91.4% of worry predictions did not come true."[13]

I rarely watch the news because it's too depressing and brings me down. The meteorologist this morning said it would be a miserable day eight times. *Eight!* Yes, it's May 2 in Michigan. We have windy, rainy days in the spring. Could she have just said the facts, that it was cold and rainy, instead of adding the adjective describing the day as miserable? She hexpected the day would be miserable for herself and told everyone else how to think about it. It confuses me how much people hexpect the weather to decide their positive outlook on life.

---

13   Lucas LaFreniere and Michelle Newman, "Exposing Worry's Deceit: Percentage of Untrue Worries in Generalized Anxiety Disorder Treatment," abstract, Behavior Therapy 51, no. 3 (May 2020): 413–423.

I shift my thoughts out of the pit of despair by approaching the future with forward-looking faith. A good friend painted on a sweatshirt for me the letters **F**antastic **A**dventure **I**n **T**rusting **H**im ("Him" meaning God). I am well aware the world is not an ideal place, but living with faith helps me see that God is in my not-yet. He is where I'm going, so I confidently and excitedly can move forward with more positive interest than fear.

When you notice the doomscrolling in your thoughts, hexpecting the worst is going to happen, start searching for what you can think about or focus on that leaves you feeling hopeful. Get busy doing something else. Take a walk. Do a word search. Write a note or send a text to someone. Flip the script and believe you can handle whatever comes your way with grace and truth to stand on.

Breaking Free from Worry—Pessimism

Example: We're going to lose everything with the way the world is going!

New Approach: We have skills and abilities to work for our food, clothing, and shelter. We can make wise decisions about how we spend our money to prepare for harder financial times.

Hex Hack:

- How much time are you spending feeding on negative information?

- What have you noticed about the way you look at the future?
- Where is your hope?

Exaggeration

I read somewhere that *exaggeration* is actually a proud word for lying.

We had amazing neighbors who let us use their pool whenever we wanted. Nice, eh? Our friends were visiting from out of town one very hot, humid weekend. Their oldest son, Alex, was probably six at the time, and when we said, "Let's go swimming," he waxed on about his amazing swimming abilities to my husband on the way to the pool. Brent believed every word. I mean, why would anyone lie about being able to swim? I doubt little Alex thought he was lying, as he probably had the idea built up in his mind that he would swan dive and nail it. It was such a surprising outcome, however, when he literally flew off the diving board into the deep end only to not come back up.

Thank the Lord Brent was there to jump in and save his bacon. When he came up sputtering chlorine out his nose and mouth, he began yelling at everyone for letting him nearly drown. The nerve! What would have happened had we not been there?

This inflated sense of self can lead us to portray something we aren't and give others a hexpectation of us.

When they find out we are devoid of said skills, character, or accomplishments, we cursed our credibility by exaggerating our personality, abilities, or beliefs. I watch it all the time. People are desperate for attention and want to fit in. They want to be included and feel like they belong to a certain social status or to find a mate. They feel like their life is dull or boring and want to sound interesting, so they make up stories. Some exaggerate their power or prestige to gain notoriety in their work. However, I coach these people. They also walk around petrified that someone might realize they're an imposter.

John Mark Comer writes, "The problem is less that we tell lies and more that we live them; we let false narratives about reality into our bodies, and they wreak havoc in our souls."[14]

I'm not going to diagnose anybody or give you ways to break all your character flaws. I'm simply asking us to notice how our thoughts lead us to do and say some excessive things. "Whoever of you loves life and desires to see many good days, keep your tongue from evil and your lips from telling lies" (Psalm 34:12–13). If your thoughts aren't lying to you, your lips won't lie to anyone else either.

---

14   John Mark Comer, Live No Lies: Recognize and Resist the Three Enemies That Sabotage Your Peace (Colorado Springs: WaterBrook, 2021), xxii.

Are you portraying something you're not so you feel better about yourself? When you have calm confidence in who you are on the inside, you don't need bigger and better exaggerations on the outside. If we never accept who we really are, we will always be exaggerating who we want to be and never be content with who we've been created to be. I found a quote by a guy named Mark Manson in a blog post. He writes, "The only way to be truly confident is to simply become comfortable with what you lack."[15]

Exaggeration sets up a hexpectation for everyone else that you will be everything you say or act you are when deep inside you know you aren't. The greatest gift we give to ourselves and others is becoming real and our realness becoming transparent, honest. The highest level of integrity is to be exactly who we are at any given moment. Not that we don't try to change ourselves and mature, but we certainly must start with who we are.

If you don't like who you are, ask yourself why and take steps to change it. There are plenty of books and blogs out there for gaining new skills and understanding. Why don't you commit to fifteen minutes a day on self-improvement?

---

15   Mark Manson, "The Only Way to Be Confident," Mark Manson (blog), accessed August 11, 2024, https://markmanson.net/how-to-be-confident.

Breaking Free from Exaggeration

Example: I'm every mother's dream for a son-in-law. I'm that amazing.

New Response: I want to be a supportive and respectful partner by treating my future wife with kindness and respect. I hope this helps foster good relations with my in-laws. I want to be well liked.

Hex Hack:

- How can you accept that the truth is cleaner than exaggerating and doesn't foster disbelief from others?

- Have you ever considered that exaggerating is the same as lying? What makes you think people need your embellishments?

- Are you afraid that people won't like or accept you if they know the real faults, fears, and shortcomings you have?

Performance

I watched the boy from a distance. He investigated the stands after every play. I didn't know what he was looking at, but I saw a man sitting, arms crossed, no emotion on his face and no words coming from his mouth. He just sat there. When strike three flew by, the boy looked into the stands again, and the man had his head hung down, shaking it from side to side.

The game ended. The team this kid played for won. My heart sank as the boy walked up to the man from the stands, who turned his back on the kid and walked off, never saying a word or making eye contact. The air was heavy around the boy as he, too, walked with his head hung low and his bat dragging behind. Another player yelled, "Hey, good game, Billy!" He looked up with a bright face and said, "Yeah! You too, Jake!"

Have you ever perceived that people, even family members, don't love you but just love what they can expect from you? They don't want your real self, just your happy, easy-to-work-with, outstanding self. If you show up with anything else, they don't know what to do with you, and you feel cursed for being who you really are.

At work, do you sense that your boss wants more than they are admitting? Or they don't seem thrilled with your ideas or suggestions but aren't being direct with you about it? Beating around the bush avoids getting to the point of a matter, but it's so unkind. Being direct doesn't need to mean being rude. It's just clear.

When others want us to be something we're not, we are forced to wear a mask. To hide what's really going on underneath, hoping nobody smells the sweat or sees our hands trembling from fear we'll be found out. We don't actually know what we're doing, and we're scared to death to admit it.

The word *performance* denotes "a show," "a production," "entertainment." How many of us are living hexhausted from hexpending copious amounts of energy pretending? But often that's what others hexpect of us. To perform. To give it our all, 110 percent. As if that's an actual calculable number. It's not.

The apostle Paul knew fully what it was to perform. Listing his credentials in Philippians 3:5–6, he could have gotten a Grammy for his Jewish performance of persecuting the new believers of Christ with his legalistic pedigree. Yet in the following verses, he counts them rubbish in exchange for being found, taken hold of by Jesus Christ himself on the cross for his sins.

Who doesn't want to be discovered? Not for our outward production but for our inner creation as a beloved person, bought with a life to know a love that surpasses knowledge or even understanding. Whew. It sends chills down my spine to believe I am loved in my deepest pain, hardest times, ugliest moments, and greatest strides of life. Nothing I do makes Christ love me more, and nothing I don't do makes him love me less. That, my friends, is so freeing.

So let the truth be told. Narcissus drowned while staring at his own reflection because he was in love with the performance of self. Similar to the selfies I see posted, people are in love with their outer appearance, and it drowns them in sorrow if they don't get any likes from others.

My audience is One—Jesus Christ, who in His very nature was God but didn't consider equality with God something to be grasped. He was humble. Nothing more attractive than a humble, confident person who lives fully but knows fully it's so not about their performance.

Breaking Free from Performance

Example: I have to make my house, family, and myself look good for so-and-so to notice and comment on how awesome we are.

New Response: We live in this house. I want to allow myself and my family the freedom to live as we are and not on a stage, pretending to be something we aren't.

Hex Hack:

- Look at the why behind what you are doing. Are you doing anything to get something or someone to notice, or are you doing it solely for your deepest self to appreciate?

- Who are you becoming something you are not for? Why? What would you prefer to have your relationship based on, performance or presence?

- In what areas do you want to change your persona for a more authentic, humbly confident self?

Fear of Aging

I entered my teen years listening to the song "Fame" that talks about living forever. It was a movie and later a television show focused on kids making it so they would be forever remembered and stay young and vibrant. Marketing strategies are constantly stating it's possible to stop the aging process by buying their product and rubbing it all over your body three times daily or taking two egg-size supplements with each meal. What happened to the idea of growing old gracefully? Why does society want me to think it's a terrible, horrible, no-good thing when a persevering man named Job said, "Wisdom belongs to the aged, and understanding to the old" (Job 12:12 NLT). His life represents the power of faith through adversity.

I always thought getting old meant having no purpose, left to rot in a nursing home. What good will I be when I'm sixty? This is a farce! Isaiah 46:4 (NLT) says, "I will be your God throughout your lifetime—until your hair is white with age. I made you, and I will care for you. I will carry you along and save you."

The hexpectation that aging is preventable and something to be feared and avoided leaves people in a lurch. We are all going to grow older, unless we die younger. That doesn't mean we need to become useless. We tend to reject the Proverb that says "Gray hair is a crown of splendor; it is attained in the way of righteousness" (Proverbs 16:31).

Maybe wrinkles are proof I've laughed, ached, and loved over a long period of time. I look to the well-worn souls of life to see what paths to take and which ones to avoid. Young people don't know what their choices will cost them in twenty or forty years.

I traveled to Taiwan to visit an exchange student we had welcomed into our home for a year. I stepped onto the train, and a random young person quickly stood up and motioned me to their seat. I wasn't even old in my mind yet (I was forty-four!). I was told Asian cultures have the most respect for the aged. I don't have to hexpect my life to be over at sixty. Heck, I read three books this summer by Peggy Rowe, who published these three books after turning eighty!

I am approaching that "older generation" stage. I've let my natural hair color (gray) illuminate my age-spotted face. I wear the necessary amount of sunscreen, but I think sunshine makes me happy.

I admire older men and women who keep themselves fit mentally and physically with fun activities, who hold hands walking down the beach, who serve their community and country in various ways. There is always someone at the grocery store who needs our friendly interaction, a baby needing arms holding it in the church nursery, and countless other volunteer agencies looking for people with listening hearts, able hands, and sage words.

"Too often, we underestimate the power of a touch, a smile, a kind word, a listening ear, an honest compliment, or the smallest act of caring, all of which have the potential to turn a life around," says Leo Buscaglia.[16]

Breaking Free from the Fear of Aging

Example: Everything in my body is going to break down, everyone around is going to die, I'm going to become a nuisance to my kids, and they'll resent me.

New Response: I can accept that my body will wear down with age, but I can nourish it well and stay active. In the circle of life, everybody does die, and I can enjoy the time we have. I can't control my kids' views, but I can choose to have a positive attitude about my life's journey.

Hex Hack:

- What are your fears around aging? There's no shame in expressing you have fear, but remaining stuck in it limits strategy and resources to help.
- Whom do you know who has aged well even if they've had physical and mental difficulties? What inspires you about their life?
- What is practically possible for you to be involved with at this stage of your life? Where can you lend a hand and reap the benefits of staying active?

---

16   Leo F. Buscaglia, Born for Love: Reflections on Loving (Thorofare, NJ: Slack, 1992), 232.

The Parenting Trap

I dreamed of being a mom for years, and I loved it. Parenting is the hardest job I've never quit. I was eager to have kiddos to love, raise, play games with, create things, teach, color with, and bake with little chubby fingers in the cookie mix.

We parented and disciplined using what we knew as the best solutions to the situations we faced. We put them in art classes, sports, music, theater. I made sure they tried all kinds of things running back and forth to school, lessons, practices, and parties. We think all these things are what make our kids into who they become. But do they? It was a hectic time of life, and we were also grateful for having the gift of children.

There are thousands of people who will tell you how to raise good kids, but each child has their own set of needs, difficulties, and demands. Internally I felt the pressure to parent well without screwing them up somehow. I felt ultimately responsible for the outcomes of our kids because someone once told me, "It's easier to build strong children than to repair broken men."[17] As a mom, I believed it must

---

17   See Aryssa Damron, "Fact Check: Did Frederick Douglass Say, 'It Is Easier to Build Strong Children than to Repair Broken Men'?" Check Your Fact, April 30, 2019, https://checkyourfact.com/2019/04/30/fact-check-frederick-douglass-easier-build-strong-children-repair-broken-men/.

be up to me to build them as strong as possible so they wouldn't break when life tossed them about.

During their teen years, I discovered I was finding my value and worth by the outcomes of their behaviors and actions. I depended on their lives turning out a certain way to make *me* feel fulfilled and happy. Although it's a right expectation of ourselves to protect our kids from evil as much as possible, our thinking that we are the god of their whole world is a hexpectation often fraught with pain and disappointment.

We guide them as best we can and pray on our knees for their protection, but our kids will work out their own journeys in time. I needed to depend on God to hold them and guide them through it while I, too, depended on God to show me what I needed to change in myself.

I redefined what made me, me. Being a mom was just one role I fulfilled, but it had taken on way too much ownership. I needed to separate myself from their results and remain clear about what my responsibilities were for myself and to them, not for them.

Breaking Free from the Parenting Trap

Example: It's my job to make sure our children turn out right.

New Response: No, it's my calling to do the best at teaching them right and wrong via the Word of God and pointing them to the One true source of all hope in Jesus Christ while loving them with grace and truth along the way.

Hex Hack:

- How are you depending on your kids for your happiness?
- What legacy do you want to leave your kids that was your focus in life?
- What are you afraid of when it comes to your kids?

Codependence

You've heard the saying "If momma ain't happy, nobody's happy," and I would add, "If nobody is happy, momma ain't happy." I was twenty-one. A counselor told me I was codependent. Heck, I couldn't even spell it, let alone understand it. However, whatever we stuff down like a beachball underwater will eventually come busting up, often giving us a black eye. I've read a lot of great books, listened to multiple podcasts, and droned through hours of talk therapy in desperate need to finally get ahold of this codependent tendency. I needed my relationships to become cleaner with my husband, our kids, and others.

Great resources exist to understand this behavior. Melody Beattie has written a few great books on the subject. Many people think codependency is just for those in a relationship with an addict. It's not. Codependency is determining our state of mind or being by how someone else is showing up in one's life. If I'm having a good day, whistling my way through cleaning the house, and my husband comes home quiet and distant, down goes my mood, and I launch into a nuclear reactor or fix-it mode to make his life better, which will make me feel better. Can you see the dangerous dance?

This is a "me problem," not a "you need to change to make me happy" solution. In recovery we say the full Serenity Prayer, which helps us stay in our lane of life. I wrote it down and posted it in my closet, car, kitchen, and bathroom. I got on my knees with the Lord and begged him to pry my fingers away from holding on too tightly to the outcomes of others. I had to stop cursing myself being their god to fix and fold and fill all their needs, pointing them to the One true source of all hope and comfort in this life and the next.

> God, grant me the serenity to accept the things
> I cannot change;
> courage to change the things I can;
> and the wisdom to know the difference.
> Living one day at a time; enjoying one moment
> at a time;
> accepting hardship as the pathway to peace;
> taking, as Jesus did, this sinful world as it is, not
> as I would have it;

trusting that You will make all things right if
I surrender to Your will;
so that I may be reasonably happy in this life,
and supremely happy with you forever in the next.
Amen[18]

Breaking Free from Codependency

Example: If I don't help them out, they're going to crash and burn. If I work hard enough at being better, he/she will be happy.

New Response: My helping can become hurtful if others do not take responsibility for themselves. I cannot change anyone else's outcome. My happiness is a choice I get to make and is not based on how others think or feel about me.

Hex Hack:

- Who are you trying to control, heavily influence, or give advice to, continuously feeling awful because they aren't changing?
- Where are you seeking constant validation: your spouse, kids, work, ministry, friends?
- Write down what you need more courage to change. What positive steps can you take to learn

---

18   Reinhold Niebuhr, quoted in "The Original Serenity Prayer by Reinhold Niebuhr," Proactive 12 Steps, https://proactive12steps.com/serenity-prayer/.

how codependency might be wreaking havoc in your life?

Stress

We took our adult kids to Mexico for a vacation to celebrate the life of Brent's dad, who passed away that summer. I picked an all-inclusive vacation destination. I even planned a few extra excursions that each individual would enjoy. This was gonna be *epic* in the middle of February to get out of the cold dreary mitten state!

The anticipation and excitement were tremendous. The stress of planning was enormous. We had never taken our kids on a trip like this before. It was fun getting summer outfits packed when snow was falling. It was delightful thinking of the poolside snacks and drinks delivered and adult children handling their own selves (gone are the diapers and wipes of yesteryear).

The flights were fantastic. The hotel van driver was friendly and engaging. While we were signing all the necessary papers, I asked, "Where are the wristbands for the meals?"

The maître d' looked at me as if I were speaking another language and said, "Pardon?"

In broken Spanglish I pointed to my wrist, making the necessary food gesture for feeding myself with a spoon.

He kindly replied in his beautiful Latin accent, "Oh, no, this not all-inclusive hotel. You pay meals separate."

I felt the blood drain from my face. I counted the number of meals and mouths we were feeding for the week in this four-star hotel. *Gulp.* Sadly, my hexpectation that this was going to be the best, most flawless vacation ever was cursed by my inability to be flexible in that moment. Suffice it to say, I worked tirelessly trying to figure out how this reality had got lost in translation at booking. I wasted a lot of emotion on this hiccup.

When planning vacations, holidays, movies, and celebrations, it's important to have realistic goals for them to be memorable. This doesn't equal flawless. Make your plans. Do your due diligence, make sure you thought of everything, and then have someone else check your list perhaps. Remember, all experiences are a journey. It doesn't have to suck when it doesn't go smoothly. There's always something to discover along the way. This could keep you from losing your marbles when the rug gets pulled out from your expectations, leaving you feeling cursed for even trying.

I listened to a friend say she just wanted to move away or go on a sabbatical, and that would fix her situation. I hastened to say, "Wherever you go, there you are." Many try running to this city or that job or have another baby or find another relationship. They discover their problems follow them. They curse everyone and everything else without looking in the mirror at who keeps following them into these situations and cities. The sooner you look at fixing your internal problem of discontentment or disconnection with yourself and your Savior, the sooner you will have the capacity to manage situations as they are, not as you hexpect them to be.

I'm certain the Israelites were so excited when Moses walked around telling them, "Shhh, get ready. We're heading to the promised land. It's gonna be awesome!" How shocked and appalled when they still needed to fend for their territory, forage for food, and find a peaceful place to sleep every day. How quickly they turned on Moses with whining and complaining.

Breaking Free from Stress

Example: My life is so busy and stressful. I can't help being frustrated all the time.

New Response: Circumstances, both positive and negative, are an inevitable part of life. We cannot choose what happens to us, but we can choose how we respond.

Hex Hack:

- Review how quickly you go from zero to one hundred, either internally or externally, when things feel overwhelming or don't go your way. What is the response you want to have in the face of adversity?

- How do these two words show up in your life: *calm* and *content*? Notice I didn't say *apathetic* or *complacent*. Look up the definitions of these words.

- When a situation is filled with stressful factors, what are three mental or physical actions you can take to stay more centered?

Perfectionism

What is it about perfectionism that traps us into thinking it's possible and that given enough determination, it's attainable? Like moths drawn to a light, perfectionism is attractive, but it is more like a prison. I always thought perfection was what made someone strong, marketable, and desirable, but no one is without imperfections physically, emotionally, or mentally. It's hexhausting always feeling uptight and defeated.

I struggled wanting to be perfect to soothe the inner ache I felt about not being enough. There never was any peace or feeling "I am enough" because the standard was unreachable. I didn't want to have any imperfections. I didn't want to feel the sting of disappointment when I came up short. This would ensure my happiness, right?

This story reflects the evidence of change that occurred in me on my journey of seeing differently and doing differently. The illusion of perfectionism was diminishing. My college friend Daniel and I worked together serving the youth of Portland, Oregon. He gave me the book

Velveteen Rabbit at the end of our school year. He said, "Thank you for showing me how to be real." It blew me away. He had observed me openly working through some hard things, trying to retrain my brain to not use negative coping behaviors. He wasn't impressed by my stylish nineties clothes or my physique on mountain bike rides. No, he thanked me for my transparency and for not letting my faults finish me. I was his living example that imperfections did not disqualify anyone from ministry or love or a happy life.

The idea that my brokenness was helpful to Dan was new for me to understand, let alone embrace. I always felt cursed for being a scatterbrain, anxious and unsure of who I was. Facing my perfectionism had to do with radical acceptance of who I was and who I wasn't. Dolly Parton said, "Find out who you are and do it on purpose."[19] Now I let my mess be a message. I have learned how to be unapologetically me while working out the character defects that keep me on my knees.

Can you be weak and feel strong at the same time? How great a chasm that lay between us and this idea of not having to do all, be all, and have it all. What a huge wake-up call for many, I presume. Paul, an apostle

---

19   Dolly Parton, quoted in "Dolly Parton > Quotes," Goodreads, https://www.goodreads.com/author/quotes/144067.Dolly_Parton.

of Jesus, could have become conceited because of his vast knowledge and revelations. However, a messenger of Satan tormented him. He begged God to release him. "But he said to me, 'My grace is sufficient for you, for my power is made perfect in weakness.' Therefore, I will boast all the more gladly of my weaknesses, so that Christ's power may rest on me. That is why, for Christ's sake, I delight in weaknesses, in insults, in hardships, in persecutions, in difficulties. For when I am weak, then I am strong" (2 Corinthians 12:9–10).

Breaking Free from Perfectionism

Example: If I don't do this perfectly, I'll lose my job, relationship, reputation.

New Approach: Nobody's perfect. There are so many good things in my life, even when I don't always see them. I am focusing on my strengths and moving forward.

Hex Hack:

- Where are you finding that your desired outcomes and reality have the most conflict? What would it look like for you to respond versus react in these situations?

- When you realize your expectations are unrealistic, how can you dial into what is tangible, doable with the situation?

- What would happen if you allowed yourself to make a few mistakes? Everyone makes them and so can you. It's okay.

Excellence vs. Perfection

Setting a high bar for our actions is not a bad thing; it will always take us to a higher plane. Striving to do better at whatever we're doing is not to be discouraged. But attempting to be perfect is a problem. I want to distinguish between trying to be perfect and seeking to be something with all the excellence we can muster. So let me digress momentarily and share Dr. Olivia Hurley's explanation of the difference:

1. Seekers of excellence typically set goals that are challenging, yet these goals remain within their reach....

2. Seekers of excellence often report feeling happier with who they are, while individuals who seek out perfection frequently state they are only happy when they consider what they have achieved on a daily basis. In other words, they base their happiness on what they do, rather than on who they are.

3. Seekers of excellence cite how they learn lessons from their defeats. In contrast, those who seek perfection often report feeling more devastated

by their defeats. The perfection-seekers frequently state they have difficulty moving on from errors or defeats....

4. Seekers of excellence are not afraid to identify their mistakes. They often view them as opportunities to learn new lessons, to establish areas for improvement in their lives....

5. Seekers of excellence tend to listen carefully to criticism, accept it, and use it as an opportunity to learn how they can do better in subsequent efforts. Perfectionists do not like or handle criticism well. They often see it as a personal attack and not as a way to help them improve on their performance efforts in the future.[20]

I was obsessed with perfection, sought validation from others, and constantly compared myself, coming up short. I wanted to control others' perception of me. I needed positive feedback to confirm my worth. Mistakes and failure were not options. I didn't realize the extent this silent obsession had then, but my future with others, God, and myself suffered.

---

20   Olivia Hurley, "Excellence Does Not Require Perfection," A Lust for Life, accessed August 11, 2024, https://www. alustforlife.com/tools/excellence-does-not-require-perfection.

While the Bible does tell us to be perfect—"Be perfect, therefore, as your heavenly Father is perfect" (Matthew 5:48)—it teaches that we cannot make ourselves perfect. Our perfection comes from God. In Hebrews 10:14 (NLT) we are told, "For by that one offering he forever made perfect those who are being made holy." Perfection is something to be received, not to be done by us. However, we are taught that excellence is something to strive for. In 2 Peter 1:5–7 (NLT), the apostle Paul says, "In view of all this, make every effort to respond to God's promises. Supplement your faith with a generous provision of moral excellence, and moral excellence with knowledge, and knowledge with self-control, and self-control with patient endurance, and patient endurance with godliness, and godliness with brotherly affection, and brotherly affection with love for everyone."

CHAPTER EIGHT

HEXPECTING OTHERS

The difference between your expectations and your experiences equals your level of satisfaction.

—DR. PAUL FRIESEN

WHEN WE ENVISION specific outcomes, setting them up in our mind for what we assume will happen exactly how we plan it, we may be casting hexpectations on others. This leaves us feeling resentful, unappreciated, or critical. When we have expectations of others that are miscommunicated or left out altogether, it causes friction in our relationships. Author Don Miller wrote, "When we can stop expecting people to be perfect, we can like them for who they are."[21]

---

21 Donald Miller, A Million Miles in a Thousand Years: How I learned to Live a Better Story (Nashville: Thomas Nelson, 2009).

Mindreading

How often do we think significant people in our lives should "just know" certain things about us? We either tell them once, hint at it, or just hope they read our minds, be it our favorite flower, restaurant, or best birthday gift. When others know details about our lives, it makes us feel special and known. There's nothing wrong with our desire, and it is healthy to pay attention to our significant relationship's unique needs. It becomes a hexpectation when we get defensive or perturbed with someone for not knowing what we are thinking or feeling. It's *inside* of *us*. Life is challenging enough just figuring ourselves out, let alone guessing at everyone else's internal journey.

Why don't we want to tell someone what we want or need? Is it less genuine when we must ask? What reaction shows up in our thoughts when people don't read the signs and follow through how we'd like them to show up?

Brent and I have dinner every night at nearly 5:30. This didn't come naturally. When first married, I worked while he attended university. He had dinner ready when I walked in the door at 5:30. I always thought this was a coincidence. Silly me. Fast forward to when we had a baby. I was working part-time, and Brent came home from work with no dinner on the table. He didn't say anything but would open and close the cupboards with some noted force and proceeded to eat a few snacks. There was this air of frustration lingering, but no words were being uttered.

I can't remember how long this went on because some days he got lucky and dinner was ready. In a huff one night he said, "Why can't we have dinner on time?"

I was astonished. What the heck did "on time" mean? To him, that meant when he walked in the door starving from a long day at work. To me, it meant when I got around to it. Somehow in the busy chaos of our lives, we didn't have the conversation about his expectation that dinner would be served close to when he got home from work.

I accept that I can please some people some of the time, but I've stopped trying to please all people all the time. I have learned how better to say what I mean and mean what I say, and how to not say it meanly; I mean I'm trying. I hear from many how scared they are to say what they really want or need from others for a variety of reasons. They have past hexperience from a spouse, parent, teacher, neighbor, child, or friend where they felt repeatedly let down or rejected. Often they pulled in or away. Dr. Spencer Johnson wrote, "Integrity is telling myself the truth, honesty is telling the truth to other people."[22] Integrity and honesty aid open-hearted discussions better than harboring the aftertaste of bitterness when they don't do what we want or think they should do.

---

22   Spencer Johnson, *Who Moved My Cheese? An Amazing Way to Deal with Change in Your Work and in Your Life* (London: Penguin, 1999).

Based on Dr. Johnson's words, I have often been dishonest with people, hoping they would just "get it." I used to beat around the bush making suggestive comments, asking questions, hoping the light bulb would go on. When it didn't, I silently sulked or, worse, acted passive-aggressively. I have learned the art of admitting what I really want. I can have kind, calm, direct conversations until greater understanding or agreement is reached with another person.

When negotiating is necessary to obtain a desired need, we must take into consideration the other person's perspective. Talking things through, we might discover our need was misplaced. Sometimes we don't need others to do things for us, but we must have the courage to do it for ourselves. No one can have all their needs met all the time. Even when we do voice them, there's no guarantee they will be met. But the probability is greater, and the internal cursing can lessen, when we feel heard.

Unspoken desires were once described to me this way: Take your right hand and hold it at shoulder height, palm down. These are your expectations. Then take your other hand and hold it waist high, palm up. This is where reality sits. The space between can often be labeled a fiasco of disappointment. If the space between isn't being talked about, this communication breakdown can lead to broken relationships. Being direct is less about confrontation and more about sharing information, which leads to greater understanding for another person to know us more intimately. I don't remember who said it, but it seems good to me.

Our lives become more peaceful when we are not looking to others to fill our emotional cups. We can turn to Jesus with our concerns and cares and ask Him to show us how to ask for our needs with the right attitude.

Philippians 4:19 says, "My God will meet all your needs according to the riches of his glory in Christ Jesus."

Breaking Free from Mindreading

Example: I hope they get me a watch for Christmas. I mentioned that mine broke the other day.

New Approach: I'm going to tell the kids I want a watch for Christmas. I can show them a few examples of what I'm thinking about. I can accept whatever they give because it's the thought that counts, or I can exchange it for one I want more.

Hex Hacks:

- What is something you know you want from someone but are struggling to say?
- How can you change your view to *sharing your wants and needs is kinder* from *hoping people guess and letting them get it wrong*?
- Who are the safest people with whom you can share your needs honestly?

Assumptions

In his book *The Four Agreements,* author Don Miguel Ruiz warns:

> The problem with making assumptions is that we believe they are the truth! We invent a whole story that's only truth for us, but we believe it. One assumption leads to another assumption; we jump to conclusions, and we take our story very personally.... We make assumptions, we believe we are right about our assumptions, and then we defend our assumptions.[23]

Our assumptions can deceive us. We are convinced they are true without any supportive evidence. We go on this rant in our head of what we think is reality, and before we know it, we are caught in a web of pure lies.

At the beginning of the book, I relayed how I assumed Brent would pick up the prescription. When he didn't pick it up, instead of checking with him about why, I made up a story in my mind to fill in the gap for what I didn't know. Filling in the situation with "He doesn't care about

---

23   Don Miguel Ruiz, quoted in Sara Smith, "Making Assumptions: A Story of Failure and Learning," International Coaching Federation, February 20, 2018, https://coachingfederation.org/blog/making-assumptions.

me" came from my own lie that says, "I am just tolerated, not loved."

The stories we tell ourselves often fuel disconnection. Imagine you are waiting for a friend to pick you up. They are late—again. You dive into the deep end of internal dialogue about how irresponsible they are and care little about anyone else but themselves. You curse their future, thinking they'll never pull it together, and you have yourself in a frenzy of frustration when you look at your phone with the ringer off. Oops, there's a text from them. They're sorry but had to pick up a prescription and would be a few minutes late. Ha.

Janessa moved to be closer to her parents when she had kids. She envisioned they would be the quintessential grandparents, doting over their grandchildren as often as possible. The reality was they didn't, and her hexpectations of them built a wall of resentment in their relationship. She had moved her entire family for this!

It took her a while to figure out it was unfair of her to assume what type of grandparents they would be based on her desires. She needed to surrender her preconceived ideas and communicate with her parents, asking what they saw as their role in her kids' lives. Then she let them know what her desires were for their involvement, and they worked through it so there was nothing hidden in what either party was expecting of the other. Eventually mutual outcomes were met because communication was open with what was desired and what was going to be given.

Try noticing how quickly an assumption forms in your head about someone or a situation. Then listen closely to the judgment that follows. There is no pause button pushed to check the facts or gather supportive data. No, just a leap to conclude the whys behind the what. This may be normal human behavior, but that doesn't make it useful or healthy.

Self-mastery is remaining figuratively still until we have all the data necessary for a complete picture to unfold. We do this by asking questions to build clarity instead of jumping to conclusions. "What are you really upset about?" can often get to the fear or disappointment underneath someone's anger they are expressing instead of assuming they are mad at you. Sometimes the emotions people express on the outside are just a cover for what they don't feel safe about or consciously realize on the inside. The gift of discernment given by the Holy Spirit has merit when reading into a situation, but it takes great skill to not jump the gun in response to it.

When we hear that voice in our head making up stories we have not vetted, we need to stop. Replace the rush to keep going down that rabbit hole of wonderland and become curious. Don't make it up. We curse the closeness we long for when we don't dare ask the obvious. We all want truthful clarity instead of creating our own versions of the truth.

Solomon wrote the wisdom books of Proverbs and Ecclesiastes. His reflections noted in this verse show he gets this idea of staying in the moment: "Fools base their thoughts on foolish assumptions, so their conclusions will be wicked madness; they chatter on and on. No one really knows what is going to happen; no one can predict the future" (Ecclesiastes 10:13–14 NLT).

Breaking Free from Assumptions

Example: My spouse is in a bad mood and is rude to me. I must have done something wrong.

New Approach: My spouse is in a bad mood. I don't need to insert a reason until they tell me one. I won't allow them to mistreat me, but I don't need to think it's my fault.

Hex Hack:

- What do you jump to conclusions about the most?
- How helpful is it to assume the worst in someone's reason for anything?
- How can you rein in your thoughts to patiently let a situation play out before you insert your own storyline of why?

If I said it, then ...

If I said it, then ... they heard it the way I meant it. Often we say something we want others to hear, believing we said it clearly and expecting the outcome will be what we think we said.

I was watching an older sitcom the other night, and the wife said, "I told you last night when you were watching the game!"

Husband: "Just because you said it out loud, doesn't mean I actually heard you!"

Wife: "You said 'Uh-huh'!"

Husband: "That was just to let you know my ears were hearing a sound coming out of your mouth!"[24]

A flippant "Hey, clean up this place before I get home" as Mom walks out the door is not clear. The "receiver" is thinking, "OK, I'll clean my room really well." They completed all the tasks they *thought* she meant. When Mom comes home and only one room has been cleaned, she gets upset because the house wasn't cleaned the way she hexpected. She yells, "I told you to clean the whole house by vacuuming, dusting, picking up toys, and making sure the dishes were put away!" No, that's *not* what was said, nor was there mutual agreement before she left the house. Basically, Mom just thought it would be done her way, which is code for "you screwed up!"

Maybe she will say nothing and be passively angry, leaving you feeling cursed. For future reference, whenever someone asks you to "clean the house," you will refer back

---

24   Everybody Loves Raymond, created by Phil Rosenthal (Burbank, CA: Warner Bros., 1996–2005).

to this situation and think, "Why should I? It won't be good enough, and I'll expend all this energy only to fail." Or worse, you will make "perfectly cleaning the house" your mantra, and anything less than that is a shame game on yourself for never measuring up. An unseen standard hangs over you from past hexperience and curses your future thoughts about "cleaning the house."

We can't hold anyone accountable for something we don't explain well. We need their confirmed agreement for the desired result to be carried out. Instructions cannot be carried out precisely unless all parties are on the same page and speaking the same language. Saying it louder doesn't equal being heard either.

Esham Hassain wrote this in a blog post:

A lot of us place unimaginable expectations on others, which is like betting on someone else's reality to match our own imagination. The odds of it being turned into our favor are ridiculously low but despite this fact, our stupid human nature hopes that it lands in our favor. Here's the honest truth about placing expectations on others, when the all too human performance of other people falls short of our own expectations, as will inevitably happen from time to time, we'll feel bitter and self-righteous.

So next time you get upset because someone else's behavior did not match your expectations, know that you are being played by your own mind because at the end of the day, you cannot control others' reality and despite this fact, placing your own happiness at the mercy of someone else's behavior is the quickest way to feel bitter and resentful.[25]

If we want someone to do something exactly, we need to say it clearly and/or write it out and ask for confirmation that they understand. They also need to agree to what we asked. If they get a bug up their nose and choose to not do it the way we asked, thereby rejecting our expectation, they can 100 percent expect there will be a disconnect in the relationship.

We need to give people the hope and firm support they need to believe they can accomplish the task. Not believing in someone's ability to do it right diminishes their belief in themselves. We need to empower others to try new things and not make it a pass/fail by our standards. Grace gives space to keep on learning.

25   Esham Hassain, "Why Do Expectations Hurt and How Can We Deal with Them?" Medium, June 20, 2019, https://medium.com/@eshamhassain4/why-do-expectations-hurt-and-how-can-we-deal-with-them-cd6d2d0029f6.

Breaking Free from "If I said it, then ..."

Example: If I leave the dishes in the sink, then someone is going to wash them and put them away.

New Approach: If I want the dishes done, I need to ask someone to do them, and they need to respond affirmatively. We need mutual understanding of outcomes for them to be fulfilled.

Hex Hack:

- What are you asking for? How clear is the mutual agreement?
- What stops you from making your requests more clear?
- Has anyone ever said you might have unrealistic expectations?

Marriage Matters

Learning healthy ways to express expectations in a relationship takes time. Marriage is a covenant partnership where two unique people learn to navigate natural differences and merge ideas, values, and passions. We work to find resolutions we both agree will be best for our relationship and situations. Choosing a partner with similar views on major issues such as religion, family, money, and politics is wise and potentially makes for a smoother union. Sadly, many of us think "the two will become one" means oneness equals sameness. The healthiest marriages have differences. It's a hexpectation to think discord is not going to show up in your marriage. It's how we handle the discord that determines the health of our relationship.

Brent and I were in our mid-twenties when we got married. We attended premarital counseling to understand the other person was not our other half to complete us. We were two independent people joining together for a fun-loving lifetime of commitment and support. But all marriages go through seasons. It was three years into our marriage when we hit a real icy patch.

We bought our first house dreaming about how to transform that ugly duckling into a beautiful swan in a snap. We both started new jobs, my dad died of cancer, I got pregnant, and progress on the house came to a crawl. We were exhausted, angry, disappointed, and disillusioned. Our biggest argument, where to put an attic access hatch, left us not speaking for days. Brent wanted it in the master bedroom. I wanted it in the hallway. We both felt unappreciated, unheard, and unwilling to change our minds. Was this really about the access hatch or something more?

We sat on opposite sides of a booth at Denny's. We tried listening without interrupting, but it was hard not to attack the other for being "wrong." I thought Brent was being deliberately slow with the remodel. He thought I was being unreasonable. Brent wanted the work done a certain way, and hiring people to do the work wasn't in the financial plan. I wanted it done so our baby wouldn't have to sleep in the bathtub. Brent was angry we weren't having as much sex as we did when first married. I was exhausted from working on the house, a full-time job, and being pregnant. I didn't even *think* about sex.

As we discussed realistic time frames and goals versus our assumed ones, I slid over to his side of the booth. Instead of talking *at* each other, we shared our perspectives *with* each other without getting defensive. I loved the idea of picking out paint colors, kitchen cabinets, and the finished project. Brent saw the whole project as therapy where he could work with his hands to deal with his stressful desk job. The access hatch wasn't the problem. It was the catalyst to discuss deeper differences we had in how we viewed life.

We started asking the right questions to better understand the other's perspective about our marriage, raising a family, work/life balance, sexual intimacy, and a host of other topics. We sat there for five hours, but it started a healthier way to approach our outlooks that were "different."

And yes, the access hatch was kindly installed in the hallway.

Many of us watch TV house flips and miracle makeovers and think, *How hard can it be?* They make it look so easy in a one-hour show, don't they? What you don't see are the arguments, exhausting hours, depleting bank accounts, and unyielding inspectors. We have done many remodels since our first one. It amazes me how the dreamy eyes of possibilities can blind us to the intensive labor it takes to transform a property.

How often do we hexpect our mate to see decisions, opinions, or situations our way? No two perspectives are the same because no two people are alike. Focusing on the differences causes misunderstanding and disconnection. Working to find common ground keeps us connected. Talking through situations with open-ended questions is helpful instead of arguing why we think that way.

Remember, all marriages need tune-ups regularly. When we were going through a difficult season as parents, we often wanted to point our fingers or get away from it all. We even went to Mexico for a vacation. I expected to get away from the chaos and rehash everything when no kids were in earshot. Brent expected that we would get away to focus on each other, have some fun, and rekindle some romance. Boy, were we fooled realizing we had brought all our problems along with us in an invisible suitcase tagged "unresolved." Once the thrill of the trip wore off on the first day, each of our hexpectations began to show up, and they were clearly not being met. It took an older couple from the UK noticing the hostile air between Brent and me to pull us out of our funk. They asked us what was so heavy between us. We shared the hurts with complete strangers, and it felt good to have their insights as they had been married much longer. They had their differences about things too, but they handled them with greater grace and respect than we were experiencing. The trip was salvaged. We enjoyed some laughter with this couple on excursions, at dinner, and dancing, and we are forever grateful.

I always think it funny when a young married couple says to me, "We get along great. We never disagree." I'm thinking, *Is one of them lying to appease the other?* Sometimes our differing perspectives are offensive when we try to force them on others.

I encourage people to use helpful questions before launching into what they want anyone to hear. "Are you open to feedback?" This gives them a choice. Instead of saying, "You always" or "You never," try saying "Sometimes when you say this, I feel like …" or "Help me understand what you are thinking when …" These approaches offer softer confrontive language rather than using accusatory words about their actions or views.

Brent and I work to get on the same side looking at the blueprints of our relationship. We've taken personality profile tests and read books. We've sat through hours of marriage conferences. It's a "we" covenant we signed up for, not a "me" marriage. We get thoughts, doubts, and issues out in the open about what we want and need. We don't leave things to chance or sweep things under rugs. Ideally, when wrong, we promptly admit it.

This isn't a book about how we have it all figured out, ya know. We are still learning to listen well and seek to understand what is driving any disagreements. We use our spoken words to communicate without hexpecting the worst from the other.

Our marriage has grown into a beautiful landscape, weeds and all, because we're learning how to use our words wisely. Proverbs 12:14 says, "From the fruit of their lips people are filled with good things, and the work of their hands brings them reward." In modern English, this means a person who speaks or thinks with wisdom will reap a harvest from their words or thoughts, just as a farmer enjoys the crops they planted.

Micah 6:8 says, "He has shown you, O mortal, what is good. And what does the Lord require of you? To act justly and to love mercy and to walk humbly with your God." Keeping these three phrases at the forefront of all our conversations will prevent cursing at each other and meet more of our expectations positively.

Breaking Free from Marital Issues

Example: Our marriage is hopeless; he/she has hurt me far too much, and I cannot see how we will ever get it right. We just think so differently.

New approach: Sadly, some marriages do need to end. Truthfully, every single person is different from any other. It takes consistency over time, and trust can be rebuilt if both of us seek to understand the other instead of making it about being right and wrong.

Hex Hack:

- What was it about your mate you admired and fell in love with in the beginning?
- Sit across from each other. One holds a spoon to dig out and share what you want the other person to hear. Pass it back to the other. Then sit next to each other and look at the situation like teammates to come up with solutions.
- What were the actions and attitudes you developed toward each other when dating or first married that need to be resurrected?

CHAPTER NINE

WE SENSE OTHERS HEXING US

The deepest fear we have, "the fear beneath all fears,"
is the fear of not measuring up, the fear of judgment.
It's this fear that creates the stress and depression
of everyday life.

—TULLIAN TCHIVIDJIAN

WE FEEL LABELED when we just can't measure up or if we always measure down to what people say about us. We feel stuck, unable to please them. There are people who will hold us at arm's length, acting cold and withdrawn, because we didn't get it right by their standards. This is how it feels to be cursed by other people's expectations.

Missing the Mark

How do we handle life when we feel like we've gotten it wrong from someone else's point of view? I first have to deal with the person in the mirror and ask, am I OK with myself and my efforts? If not, how can I own my shortcomings? Nobody's perfect. I find people who have little grace for themselves have little ability to offer it to others. No one answers for me. I may not have control over anyone else, but I do have control over my responses.

If we are always trying to measure up (or down) to other people's expectations, insecurity will prevent us from hitting the bullseye. We've all walked into certain situations, maybe a board meeting, and wondered, *What do I do now? How should I act? What should I say? Am I what everyone expects me to be?* This is such a game. We do it because we've all met people who keep a scorecard. When we do something right by them, we get points. When we do something they disapprove of, we get strikes. We've experienced getting it wrong by other people's standards or opinions. They shun us, exclude us, shut us out, and criticize us for being different. Until we do good things that meet their approval, they won't remove the pin of punishment from our lookalike doll.

Unspoken issues others have with us are not our responsibility. We don't play pin the tail on meeting everyone's expectations. If we sense there is a disconnect, we can ask for clarification. If they refuse to *go there*, that's on them. It's our choice whether their disappointment leaves us feeling small and insignificant. If the relationship is one that deserves taking the conversation to the next level, we attempt to do so kindly and with clarity. Or we let it go until the Lord directs a possible meeting.

We can change how negative opinions from others affect us when they think we have missed the mark.

Breaking Free from Missing the Mark

Example: I wonder why my good friend Sally won't return my texts or phone calls anymore. What could I have done?

New Approach: First, I'm going to pray for discernment. Wait for the appropriate time, and ask Sally if she is open to a conversation about the distance between us.

Hex Hack:

- Who are you constantly thinking you are letting down for not measuring up to their standard of unspoken or unrealistic hexpectations?
- How can you gain better clarity regardless of whether this is true, or are you assuming it's based on their behavior toward you?
- What next step do you want to take to "go there" and find out how you can close the gap in your relationship that feels out of sync?

Sexpectations

Sex is one of the highest levels of communication we can have with another, but it also can cause some of the deepest pain. I do not intend to solve people's issues in the bedroom, let alone in any other area of life. However, this section is about shining a spotlight on the unspoken and unrealistic sexpectations we might be carrying into our sexual relationships. I know there are many misconceptions and much chaos around this subject. I don't want to avoid it because of the tension. I trust you can take what you need from this chapter.

I know countless numbers of both men and women who have been abused. I am deeply, so very sorry you have gone through that awful experience. There is no doubt it has left an indelible mark on your psyche. I've experienced sexual abuse, so I understand it's complicated. However, in the right context and with quality help, people can change.

I've heard it said that men say, "I love you" to get sex and women have sex to hear "I love you." Brent used to think doing the dishes would guarantee sex that evening. Sadly, he often felt unfulfilled because I equated doing dishes with just part of household chores. I was never handed the code book for "If I do this, then sex is the reward." However, I'm told it exists … in men's minds. Most men would love the idea of having sex whenever they want it. Likewise, some women silently expect their men to romance them every day like they did at the beginning of their relationship. Neither of these desires is wrong, but are they being communicated effectively to be fulfilled consistently? Sadly, I think both men and women desire what they see on the movie screen or in their daydreams but feel what they have in their bedroom is ho-hum. I'm simply trying to say both men and women have sexpectations we're not talking about.

Earlier, I shared that *unrealistic* has a synonym called *romantic*. Some of us have read magazines and steamy romance novels and watched sexually explicit content smeared with images that can taint reality. Maybe you have listened to others brag about their hot sex on the weekend. These behaviors all work to fuel the idealistic, illusory, imaginary sexual intimacy Hollywood or Satan would want you to think is what love-driven sexual experience is about.

So many couples just don't talk about it. I used to think anything sexual was dirty and taboo because people treated the subject with crass and off-putting language. That God didn't want us talking about it, let alone *doing it*. What a lie! Personally, I believe sex can be a grace-filled appreciation for the God-*created* act of intimate relations between a husband and wife. I believe God wanted us to enjoy a grace-filled sexual experience; why else would he give a woman a clitoris and a man a penis head? He could have made this act strictly physical. But He didn't. Sex was intended to cause us to procreate and fill the earth. However, doesn't it also draw us closer emotionally, physically, and relationally? This is one of the biggest areas where relationships die with unfulfilled desires. We all approach this from very different perspectives and possibly even past painful experiences.

Investigating the genesis of sex, we see the man and his wife were created naked, inspired to become one flesh and to *feel no shame*. Who is the ultimate deceiver of hexpectations around sex? Satan. Once Adam and Eve turned their eyes and ears to listen to the serpent woo them into disobeying God's explicit order to not eat from the tree of the knowledge of good and evil, they became defiled and ashamed. Genesis 4:7 shows us, "Sin is crouching at your door; it desires to have you, but you must rule over it." The implication here is we *can* master sin through the power of a redemptive relationship with Jesus Christ, who bore our sin and shame on the cross. We cheapen this amazing gift of holy sex given by God to husbands and wives when we step away from God's design.

A common scenario is when a person dates someone who is hot and ready all the time, can't wait to fool around together, and always does their hair, makeup, and dresses to the nines. Once married, however, it is a bait and switch. After the honeymoon wears off, she is not interested sexually anymore. He feels disappointed beyond belief, even hexed, like he was in a trance of romance and now reality has hit him like a glass of cold water. This can go both ways.

It takes mutual understanding and agreement for there to be ultimate satisfaction, right? But where might you be hexpecting your partner to just read your cues or your mind or assume what you want if you aren't talking about it consistently? This is not a one-and-done arena of your relationship. Ideas can be discussed, positions changed. Things that used to work might not work as well later in the relationship.

If someone is hexpecting you don't want sex, cursing you because the last time they wanted it, you got a headache or blew them off, they are feeling jilted before they even ask. Cursed for wanting it, hexed for not getting it.

Brent and I would say we have a great sex life. You know why we call it great? Because both of us are satisfied, pleased, and fulfilled. It's not because we are "getting it on" daily or in risky places, or that it's always exciting. But all those things have happened at one time or another. Frankly, in our fifties, it's happening less frequently but with the same outcome: genuine, life-giving love expressed sexually with each other. Our spouses are designed by God for mutual enjoyment.

How can you experience sexual intimacy with your spouse that stands the test of time and trials? I think it starts with being honest. Start with the basics of what you do or don't want. Talk about it. Write it down in a letter. Start emailing each other to initiate the conversation if face-to-face feels uncomfortable at first. Get a third party involved if necessary to make sure hijacking of the conversation doesn't happen by one or both of you.

Whatever you do, make sure your own heart and mind are clean before God before approaching the relationship.

A great book on this subject is *Beyond the Battle: A Man's Guide to His Identity in Christ in an Oversexualized World*. It is not just a man's battle, and women reading this book can absorb the truths for themselves. Please don't assume the other should *just know,* even after many years of marriage. Remember, love in its basic form "is patient … [and] kind. It does not envy, it does not boast, it is not proud. It does not dishonor others, it is not self-seeking, it is not easily angered, it keeps no record of wrongs. Love does not delight in evil but rejoices with the truth. It always protects, always trusts, always hopes, always perseveres" (1 Corinthians 13:4–6).

Breaking Free from Sexpectations

Example: Maybe if I get her flowers and take her to a lovely dinner, I'll get sex tonight.

New Approach: I'm going to get her flowers, enjoy dinner out together, and let her know my desire is to end the evening sexually celebrating our marriage. Then ask if she thinks that sounds like something she would enjoy as well.

Hex Hack:

- What unresolved experiences or thoughts around sexual intimacy may need to be addressed for you to express this area of your life more freely?

- How can you normalize the subject of sexual intimacy realizing God created it to unite a couple on a level they cannot, nor should, receive from anyone else?

- What is one thing your partner does, as a person you admire, that fuels your desire to make loving them important, in a way they can see and feel?

Labeling

Sticks and stones can break bones, but words and labels can sear our soul and spirit. We have all heard a word spoken over us that stung. When we close our eyes, we can see the person's face who said it or feel the sting when slapped by the biting words. When a person hears they are lazy or complicated or will never amount to anything, it leaves a stain on their brain. We feel saddled with this label, and it follows us everywhere like a dark shadow. We become incarcerated in our minds. Whether said once or a thousand times, our thought structures are altered when we are told things that cut to the heart of who we are.

These types of phrases attach themselves to the mirror we look into. Whenever we try to advance, we retreat from an invisible wall that stops us, saying, "Nope, can't do that ... remember, I'm a loser, stupid, ugly." We then play out of that narrative, and we believe everyone thinks of us this way because we think of ourselves this way.

My friend's dad called her a "fat ass" growing up. His focus on negatively labeling her outward appearance left her belittled. She felt her body was cursed and hexpected she would never be beautiful in a man's eyes. This drove her to use anorexic behaviors, working to stay skinny, believing that was what all men wanted. She was desperate to gain her father's affirmation by staying a certain size.

She carried this label into her adulthood in other ways by continuously focusing on her external features. She was careful what clothes she wore and how they hung on her body, how her hair was styled, and that her makeup was always in place. She never felt confident that the inner beauty formed in her by God's loving hands was enough to warrant people's approval.

The opposite kind of label can damage a person as well. Labeling the accolades and outstanding characteristics of a child can place pressure on them they might not understand but feel daily: the favorite child, the easy child, the smart child.

Melanie was labeled highly intelligent and studious because she enjoyed learning. This separated her from her peers, who used her uniqueness as fodder to chastise her. She grew up thinking being smart was a curse rather than a blessing because it left her feeling alone from the rest of the kids at school.

We all know those prodigies who show the same interest in a parent's profession or favorite sport. The next step is they are hexpected to attend the same college, pledge to the same fraternities, and sign up for the same extracurriculars. Kids are left floundering trying to find what is inside them for their own journey onto whatever path they choose but feel cursed if they step outside what they've always been told they must do.

I walk beside people with addictions and compulsive behaviors at Celebrate Recovery, which is a Christ-centered twelve-step recovery ministry. People attend our meetings feeling saddled by their addiction of choice, having been labeled addict, hopeless, incapable of freedom from alcohol, drugs, porn, depression, raging anger, anxiety, food. All sorts of labels walk through our doors. The chain of shame is heavy around the necks of those who have tried to get free but failed.

If people stick around long enough, they will hear someone say they are a grateful believer in Jesus who has victories yet still struggles. They also will hear how others have peeled off the negative labels they couldn't remove on their own. It's the power of Jesus that transforms their lives when they surrender. I always encourage people to memorize Scripture because it is the best label-removing source out there. Hebrews 12:1 says, "Therefore, since we are surrounded by such a great cloud of witnesses, let us throw off everything that hinders and the sin that so easily entangles. And let us run with perseverance the race marked out for us."

Just because someone says it, doesn't make it true. Labels can often feel like something heavy and dark has been thrown over us, preventing light from shining through. Discovering the weight of the words, we get to choose to take it off. "Like a fluttering sparrow or a darting swallow, an undeserved curse does not come to rest" (Proverbs 26:2).

Breaking Free from Labeling

Example: She said I was a terrible mother.

New Approach: Sometimes I have acted terribly as a mom. I can own my mistakes. I have confessed and worked to change them; I am not altogether good, but I am not altogether a terrible person either.

Hex Hack:

- What phrase or name comes to mind that you have been told or called and feels stuck on you?
- How often have you labeled yourself or someone else with a label that felt sticky and you couldn't get it off?
- How can you relabel yourself with ten positive traits? When negative labeling starts nagging in your mind, write three things down you are good at to silence the inner critic.

The Challenge of Living by Others' Expectations

I found that this article from the Manhattan Health Counseling Agency fairly gauges the weight we place on the desires we feel from others. I interspersed some of my own thoughts throughout as well.

Why do the expectations of other people create such inner conflict in our lives? The reasons are many, but let's just look at a few:

- **Expectations are not an accurate gauge of what is right for you**. Even with the best of intentions, someone else's expectation of you will be based not on who you are, but on that person's own experience, opinions, pain, disappointments, and moral values. In other words, those expectations aren't really about you—they're about the other person. Accordingly, they're not necessarily a good compass for your life.

- **Expectations are often unrealistic**. Because expectations are devices of the mind, they are often not grounded in reality. They don't take into account your abilities or your desires, or even what is possible or reasonable. When you try to live up to unfair expectations, you'll fail every time.

- **Expectations are contradictory**. Most of us have more than one person of influence in our lives, and since no two people have the same perspective, the expectations of these people will inevitably contradict at some point. It's statistically impossible to please everyone at once, so when you live to please others, you'll be faced with continual failure.

Living by others' expectations can be harmful.

No matter how hard we try, we cannot avoid living with expectations, ours and those of others. Expectations are unavoidable, but when we internalize them the wrong way, it can affect us negatively in a number of ways.

- **It can breed anger and resentment**. The saying goes: "Expectations are premeditated resentments." It doesn't just breed resentment in the person whose expectations we fail to meet—it breeds resentment in us, as well. When we deny our own desires in favor of the expectations of others, we are prone to become resentful or angry.

- **It can cripple our own ability to make decisions**. Ronit Baras is an educator, life coach, author, journalist and international speaker who has been teaching emotional intelligence techniques for thirty-three years around the world. She refers to this as our "wanting muscle." When we allow the voices of others to drown out what we want for ourselves, we lose the ability to have an opinion, and our self-esteem plummets.[26]

- **It can lead to mental health issues like depression**. Psychologist Lara Honos-Webb, PhD, says living a life driven by a need for approval leads to inner conflict and ultimately depression. "The more conflicted you feel, the more afraid you become of expressing your real self," she says. "As a result, you may drive your feelings deeper underground."

- **Expectations are powerful**. When they are unmet, they lead to disappointment, frustration, and often anger. Proverbs 13:12 says, "Hope deferred makes the heart sick, but a longing fulfilled is a tree of life." None of us want to be sick and tired, but that's the result when our hopes get dashed on the rocks of unmet expectations. When our realistic desires get fulfilled, it's because we took the same effort likened to growing a tree. We need adequate time and space to plant,

---

26   See Ronit Baras, "The Want Muscle," Family Matters (blog), last modified December 25, 2019, https://www. ronitbaras.com/emotional-intelligence/personal-development/want-muscle/.

water, fertilize and prune in order for growth to occur.[27]

Satan tries to back us into a corner thinking it's the end of the world if we let anyone down ... but it's never been my job to hold them up. Jesus held the key to set me free from myself and the tyranny of Satan when he crushed the serpent's head on Calvary and said, "It is finished." All the striving, obsessing, planning, coercive efforts to make sure things would work out for everyone around me could cease now.

I always wanted to take a vacation from myself. But wherever I went, there I was. I learned how to survive the pressures I felt within, but I hadn't learned how to live until I fully realized Jesus said I could come to Him as I was and not how everyone wanted me to be.

Nevertheless, we should be mindful that what we expect of ourselves and others has powerful potential.

---

27   Natalie Buchwald, "How to Let Go of the Expectations of Others," Manhattan Mental Health Counseling, updated June 3, 2023, https://manhattanmentalhealthcounseling. com/how-to-let-go-of-the-expectations-of-others/. Reprinted by permission of Natalie Buchwald.

BREAKING HEXPECTATIONS

CHAPTER TEN

BRIDGING THE GAP

The biggest gap in your life
is between what you know and what you do.

—BOB PROCTOR

HEXPECTATIONS CAUSE US to step back from an adventurous life and live a fearful, caged existence. We often retreat from relationships rather than advance toward deeper connections because we cannot overcome the disappointment when the expectations go unmet. If we think negatively, we will act negatively. We will act positively if we think positively. We must become radically aware that our thoughts drive our actions and behaviors.

If you've come to this point in the book realizing you have hexpectations, what do you want to do about it? Don't get hung up thinking this is just one more thing you do wrong and you're never gonna have it all together. However, when we are more aware of our pitfall mindsets, we can change them, which transforms our outcomes.

Change. It's a verb meaning, "1. To make or become different. 2. To replace with another."[28] How do we take what's in our head, change it, and do life differently?

Actress, singer, and writer Portia Nelson tells of her life in a five-part short poem titled "There Is a Hole in My Sidewalk." She opens with a description of falling into a hole in the sidewalk and not knowing how that happened. She feels powerless and confused. She can't see a way out. It takes her a very long time to climb up from the pit. In the next stanza, she takes the same path but ignores the hole in the sidewalk and still falls in. She's surprised it happened again but doesn't believe she's at fault. She feels stuck and it takes her a long time to get out. The next time she sees the hole but falls in anyway. Now she recognizes her culpability. She is alert, sensible, and scrambles out of the hole right away. The next line, she steps around the hole. In the final chapter, she chooses to take a different street.[29]

Look up the poem and read it. I hope you marvel at how simple she makes transformation sound.

When the phrases "I can not" and "I will not" turn into "I can" and "I will," the traction to change begins.

---

28 Merriam-Webster, s.v. "change (v.)," accessed August 12, 2024, http://www.merriam-webster.com/dictionary/change.

29 "Autobiography in Five Short Chapters" from Portia Nelson, *There's a Hole in My Sidewalk: The Romance of Self-Discovery* (1993; repr., New York: Atria, 2012), xi–xii.

Change takes progressive, honest self-reflection, making minor adjustments consistently. I had a habit of overreacting and letting my emotions drag me down. This poem reminds me I do have choices in how I respond to life's circumstances and everyone around me. However, habits are powerful. We need to be gentle with ourselves. Change takes time.

What's the hole in your sidewalk? Your temptation, difficulty, mindset, weakness that swallows you whole. How can you take personal responsibility? How can you let something go, maybe even forgive someone who didn't ask for it. You can choose to walk down a different path of behavior.

We must learn to magnify what is most important, minimize what's not, and figure out the difference by the results felt and known by all parties involved. "Complacency is a state of mind where people become satisfied with their current level of success and stop striving for improvement. It is a dangerous trap that many people fall into, because it limits their ability to reach their full potential and stifles their success." [30]

Too often we get so comfortable in our thinking cage (brain) that we begin to hang pictures making it home.

---

[30]   Zach Sabin, "4 Ways Complacency Stifles Your Success and How to Prevent It," LinkedIn, February 27, 2023, https://www.linkedin.com/pulse/4-ways-complacency-stifles-your-success-how-prevent-zach/.

Instead, we should stop normalizing a negative behavior we grew up with or have grown accustomed to and find out what healthy living can feel like.

CHAPTER ELEVEN

MY PERSONAL BREAKTHROUGH

The mental act of expecting something
often gives us the illusion of control.

—NICK WIGNALL

LIFE CAN BE hard to ride. There's no crystal ball to tell us how situations will turn out, which causes some of us incredible anxiety. My relying less on God and more on *my* ability to make all things work together for good was weighing heavy in my mind as a parent and woman. I'm going to describe what brought me to the point of dealing with the silent, negative narrative that finally came to a breaking point.

Our church wanted to start a Celebrate Recovery for people with hurts, hang-ups, and habits. I was very public with my journey of overcoming eating disorders and other addictive behaviors. I've facilitated groups about recovery for years. So my church asked me to attend the annual recovery summit to gather information. My mask said I looked like I had it all together. I did have some issues worked out in my life. However, silently, I often still had these loathing, damning conversations with myself when I felt less than perfect. I would beat myself up for the simplest mistakes and for not feeling good enough.

I was living a fiasco of crazy at home with three teens demonstrating their independence in ways that could turn horribly wrong at any given moment. I felt so much pressure to raise good kids God's way ... or my way. I got the two mixed up sometimes. Kids have a mind of their own and will make messy choices. I thought if I was a good enough mom, our kids "will soar on wings like eagles; they will run and not grow weary, they will walk and not be faint" (Isaiah 40:31). Oh, wait. That's if they trust in the Lord, not me.

I was just not feeling like the fun, supportive mom I'd been during the younger years and didn't know how to handle the opposition I felt. This stage of parenting was not turning out how I hexpected, and my heart and head were in pain.

I was also experiencing an emotional roller coaster with my hormones. I had never heard the word *perimenopause*. Doesn't *peri* mean "near or around," and *menopause* means our female cycles get easier? I thought this chapter of life after having and chasing babies was supposed to be where

I came into myself and had life figured out. No, this was different.

For fourteen days in my cycle, I thought life was great. The next fourteen felt like I was falling into a dark abyss. I had little control of this hormone-induced emotional and mental shift. It happened month after month, but I wasn't telling anyone how desperate I felt. I hated being human, and the thought "Everyone would be better off without me" whispered in my ear again.

I agreed to attend this summit in Tennessee. On my way to the location, someone rear-ended me on the highway. My neck felt pretty sore from the impact. Plus, I got a call that my teenager had skipped school again.

"Why am I even at this conference? Nobody knows how much I hate my life right now."

God knew.

A sweet woman handed me my summit bag of goodies, and maybe she noticed the internal ranting on my external face. She asked warmly, "Are you OK?"

My reply, "Yeah, just a bit flustered," was an understatement.

I made my way to a seat in the back of the auditorium. This guy sitting beside me said I was in his friend's seat. I didn't see a sign but let my sarcastic thoughts stay in my head.

I moved. That internal voice sneered: "I swear I'm cursed. Something always goes wrong when I'm involved." I looked at the theme, "Come as You Are," on the front of my notebook, nametag, and on the stage.

Being a wife and mom was both rewarding and demanding. Kind of like getting a deep-tissue massage. It hurt so good. I loved being a mom. I had this romantic picture of how I wanted my house, marriage, kids, job, vacations, and relationships to go. I thought we were that family that could escape all the hard issues I often saw. However, these unrealistic hexpectations were making it hard to stay positive.

I was thinking there would be no come-as-you-are for me because I must be better, do better, feel, look, and act better than everyone around me. I wasn't.

As the conference started, a video played of this kind couple trying to rescue a little dog covered in scabs and open sores, cowering under a car. Then he ran down the streets and alleys until they had him backed into a corner. He lashed out, biting the handler. How could he understand he was living a life filled with unnecessary pain and fear when a better life was available?

The video ended and the band sang a David Crowder song titled "Come As You Are." It's about getting away from the places where we've been buried by painful circumstances. We're never in too deep for God. Divine restoration begins when we bow down before the Lord and leave our troubles at His feet. Then our souls can have peace and rejoice in Him. All we need to do is relax in Jesus's embrace and offer Him our hearts, just the way they are.[31]

While singing, tears fell down my face as I became acutely aware I was hiding how I really felt about myself and my roles as a woman, mom, wife, daughter, sister, neighbor, and friend. I didn't think God would be pleased with my messiness, but He wanted me to break the curse of silence. I found a leader at the summit who listened to my pent-up, disparaging thoughts. I felt liberated when she said, "Thank you for sharing." She didn't offer to fix me, tell me what to do next, or preach at me. She asked me a few reflective questions about what I wanted to do with this new awareness. She encouraged me to believe in the changes God would make as I surrendered my will over to His care and control, which is step three in the twelve steps of recovery.

---

31   Crowder, "Come as You Are," Neon Steeple, 2014, Sixstepsrecords.

CHAPTER TWELVE

MY
SELF-AWARENESS

An unhappy man wants distractions—
something to take him out of himself.

—C. S. LEWIS

"LIFE IS DIFFICULT" [32] is the opening line of one of the first books I read in my early Christian life. How brilliant to say it so plainly. When we accept that life *is* difficult, that nobody gets a free pass of sweet and easy, we can develop the tools to cope and move forward with that concept. Realizing everyone has problems takes the air out of my whining "Why isn't it easier for me?" I started seeing how I was setting myself, my kids, my husband, my job, and God up with unspoken, unrealistic tight parameters of how things must be for me to be

---

32   M. Scott Peck, *The Road Less Traveled*: A New Psychology of Love, Traditional Values and Spiritual Growth (New York: Simon & Schuster, 1978), 15.

happy. It was completely unfair and caused disconnection in my relationships.

I returned from the recovery summit with this new awareness. I began seeing a counselor who helped me face what I could and couldn't control in myself and others. I admitted to my husband and a few friends where my dark thoughts were taking me. I didn't complicate my life by using any addictive or damaging compulsive behaviors to run away from my feelings. I'd been down that road and knew it was a dead end. I felt every feeling and faced every thought of fear with the faith of a mustard seed. Slowly that seed grew.

I became a leader for our church's Celebrate Recovery ministry, which meets fifty-two weeks a year. Step one: I admitted I was powerless over my compulsive negative thinking and that my life had become unmanageable. Every other Monday night in large group, we hear testimonies from people who have changed their thoughts, which changed their choices. Biweekly, somebody shares great teachings on denial, hopelessness, action, and turning our lives and compulsive behaviors over to the care of God.

A smaller assembly called Open Share meets after the large group. It's a free space where we speak out in a circle, uninterrupted. Nobody judges or asks us questions about how our emotions, thoughts, and behaviors are hijacking our peace.

I started admitting I wanted to die, escaping the fear of the unknown. I dove deeper into the codependency issues, disappointment, and anger choking out my joy. I got busy figuring out how to manage my emotions positively instead of letting them mismanage me. I allowed the Truth of God's Word to be the doorkeeper of my thoughts, locking the good ones in safe and sound while breaking the cycle of the negative ones.

I am living a renewed life because I talk about the tightening grip my thoughts sometimes have on me and how they affect my actions and expectations. I get into the light, although Satan wants me to keep in the dark. I ask God daily to search me and know my heart. For Him to test me and know my anxious thoughts. I ask if there is any offensive way in me and to lead me in the way everlasting (see Psalm 139:2; 23–24).

I know our outcomes are in Jesus's hands, especially our kids. I do not need man's approval or seek the world's direction. I'm ordering my private and public world to focus on God's presence, which keeps me centered.

Debra Rickwood, professor of psychology at the University of Canberra and head of research at Headspace National Youth Mental Health Foundation, says:

> The reason that beliefs and expectations affect outcomes in our lives is because they influence how we behave; it is not just the thought, but

how that thought affects our subsequent behavior that matters. If we think we can achieve something, we are likely to put in the necessary effort, problem-solve to overcome barriers, and persevere till we get the outcome we set out to obtain.

However, reality imposes its own limits and positive expectations, and hard work doesn't always win out. For every story of someone who persevered against extraordinary odds, there are those people who foolhardily continued down a path to their demise. Sometimes the hardest decisions to make in life are whether to try harder or walk away.

Nevertheless, we should be mindful that what we expect of ourselves and others has a powerful potential.[33]

This is an invitation to embark on your own self-awareness journey. Take a break. Set the book down. Lean back in your chair or walk away and observe the

---

[33]   Debra Rickwood, "Can Expectations Really Affect Reality?" Business Chicks. This article is no longer available, but you can find an archived version here: https://web.archive.org/web/20230929081432/https://businesschicks.com/the-expectation-effect/. Quoted with permission.

impact your internal expectations have on your psyche and your relationships. Do you feel uptight? Let down? Disappointed? Cursed?

Recovery says step one is about becoming aware. Ending the denial that we all hex our expectations a time or ten is enlightening and empowering. Admission has conditions we now change. A friend said to me the other day, "We cannot do better until we become better." Better at noticing, becoming curious how to reframe our thoughts so our expectations follow more healthfully toward ourselves and others.

I am thankful God tells us in Scripture, "Come to me all you who are weary and burdened and I will give you rest. Take my yoke upon you and learn from me for I am gentle and humble at heart, and you will find rest for your souls. For my yoke is easy and my burden is light" (Matthew 11:28–30).

CHAPTER THIRTEEN

BREAKING THE CURSE

If you don't like something, change it; if you can't
change it, change the way you think about it.

—MARY ENGELBREIT

WRITING HEXPECTATIONS HAS been cathartic, pushing me to
notice how often I don't speak clearly and make assumptions
about people, situations, the gamut. I'm learning to purge the
negative narrative out of my head, making clear what I want,
need, and desire with and for myself.

If you're feeling like a prisoner of your own mind, I want
you to know that you're not alone. Changing our hexpectations
isn't easy. Finding freedom takes a lot of time and effort. I have
started to break free from my brain cage and feel more confident
and positive. I am learning to let go of obsessive control and
just enjoy life. And I am experiencing a great amount of peace
from the changes.

When I discovered this idea of hexpectations, fireworks
went off in my brain. I would catch myself internally prewriting

how situations were going to play out. I would hear entire conversations with other people's voice-overs that I was having inside my head. If I was going to bring up a hard topic with someone, I would have their reaction already built up in my mind. These things had to change.

I've learned to speak more directly, with grace and a fair amount of healthy humor, not taking myself too seriously. I keep it balanced. I use concise, kind words that are clearer, which has freed me from the debilitating dysfunction of negativity that used to dance around me. I'm telling you, there's no sound louder than a captive set free!

My mind is most secure when I hold on loosely to outcomes and don't let go of living God's way every day. When I cling too tightly to my way, I lose control (yes, the 38 Special song is my influence here). Texas Stready wrote a great memoir called *Deep in the Heart of Texas*. Hers is a story of breaking free. She recently posted, "Stop holding on to illusions you want to be true and accept what's really happening."[34] A good word about living in reality. There's incredible peace when we find a way to let go of the tight grip of having expectations be what we hexpect them to be and embrace a life of surrendering to outcomes that could

---

34   Texas Stready (@TexasStready), "Stop holding on to illusions you want to be true and accept what's really happening," Instagram, July 1, 2024, https://www.instagram.com/p/C84KwToKcVj/.

be for our good, if we let them. Don't forget, "Let it be" was a phrase that made millions in the 1960s.

Learning the art of saying what we want out loud instead of just thinking and hoping people read our mind brings us closer to having our expectations heard and reasonably met. Gaining perspective on what we accept as achievable prevents unrealistic perfectionism from saying nothing is ever good enough. Let's not live with wishful thinking, hoping for the best. We can have better results or meet expectations if we speak up and say what we want and how we want it. Speaking up is not demanding our expectations be met. It's communication 101 with being clear, concise, and caring with our words. Then we continue the dialogue until mutual understanding and agreements are in place, ensuring the outcome will be closer, if not exactly what we hoped it to be in the first place.

I believe most things come down to a powerful word— *choice*. We break away from bad habits, old patterns, and mindsets when we become aware and then choose differently.

In my mind there are four things we need to focus on to break free from cursing our expectations from being met: Clarity, Trust, Release, and Hope.

Clarity

We need to say what we want and need for ourselves and from other people and situations. Not in a demanding "it's got to be this way or else" tone either. This is not beating around the bush or using a facade hoping someone gets your drift. Don't get sucked into the idea that if someone really loves you, they'll just know what you want.

Trust

Yes, it takes time to communicate distinctly and change how we think. Trust the process. Consistency over time builds trust. This is not a one-and-done change. I so wanted to hang up a banner for my family that said, "HEY, I'm changing here, do you notice?" Trust they will notice as you remain faithful to the process of change.

Release

Let go of internal negativity, pessimism, projecting, assuming, and unrealistic ideals. I've lived with these seemingly obscure forces I held against myself, and I'm learning how to expose and release them. Learn to live in the now and let the not-yet be held by God until you get to it, knowing that together with God, consistency, and time, you will figure it out when you get there.

Hope

The avoidance of hope is a type of protection against being hurt. Some people are afraid to hope because they have been hurt so much in life. They've had so many disappointments; they don't think they can face the pain of another one. They simply refuse to believe that anything good will ever happen to them. Therefore, they refuse to hope so they won't be disappointed. This type of behavior sets up a negative lifestyle.

Our hope for the future motivates us in the present. How often I have tried to start a fire God wasn't lighting, hoping he would get with the program. Now my hope is less about what I'm expecting to get and more about possessing calm confidence about my life in the now. Having a daily walk with Jesus Christ fuels my confidence He will guide me, versus living in the fury of fretting. It's about that still, small voice in my soul whispering Romans 12:12, "Be joyful in hope, patient in affliction, faithful in prayer."

CHAPTER FOURTEEN

CREATING NEW SKILLS

Success is 20 percent skills and 80 percent strategy.
You might know how to read, but more importantly,
what's your plan to read?

—JIM ROHN

YEARS AGO, I took a self-defense class to learn how to break away from someone's harmful hold on me physically. I learned new skills and practiced them repeatedly with the instructor coming at me from different directions. Likewise, this chapter summarizes how to break away from the psychological cursing you feel in yourself or from others, or from those chokeholds you may be placing on people in your life.

Develop Realistic Expectations Eliminating Resentments

It is not enough to just eliminate false or unrealistic expectations. We need to develop a strategy of creating expectations that are realistic and helpful. Making sure you are living with real expectations starts with accepting what is factual, sensible, and practical. Start with what is real and not with what you expect to be real. The path to change takes some time and effort, but the following tips may help you get started:

- **Cultivate your inner voice.** Take some time alone and sincerely ask yourself what you want (journaling your thoughts often helps). If no one else was telling you what you should want, what would you want for yourself or a situation? I'm working at being kind to me for being plain ole me. Sometimes I have all cylinders firing. Sometimes I don't, but I am loved and OK either way. No judgment on my outcomes. Reflection yes, but condemnation is not for anyone who finds themselves living with Christ seated on the throne of their life.

- **Look for the positives** in what you already have. Beware of believing that once you have obtained what you expect, you will be completely happy. Be reasonable about what is doable for the average human being.

- **Accept that life is difficult** but not impossible. Expecting life to be smooth and easy is catastrophic to the reality that things like sickness, death, accidents, job loss, etc. happen all the time. Balancing the knowledge that there will be trouble in life with the power to persevere in them through the power of the Holy Spirit living within you as a follower of Christ is key.

- **Begin saying what you want out loud.** Be affirmative, not defensive, but get in the habit of expressing your opinions, wants, and needs. They're as valid as anyone else's.

- **Check your own expectations of others.** When you find yourself assuming someone should "just know," stop. Send the text, write the note, and gain their full attention and mutual agreement about what you want with or from them.

- **Loosen your expectations of self and others.** Basic life care, holidays, and family get-togethers can be less stressful if we don't set them up to be supernatural. If Uncle Johnny is usually a jerk, believe he could change, but don't get hung up if he doesn't. If your mother-in-law is always rude, know she might have a shining moment and believe for it, but don't run out the door if she shows up the same as always. If God is your shield, let His words stop hers that feel piercing and say, "She just doesn't know any better ... yet." Stay open to the possibility she could change as you stay off the swing of hexpecting it to always be awful or that things should only go how you want them to.

The way I cure having hexpectations is to let people off the hook of my desired outcomes for them. Let them live their lives and make their mistakes, know my lane, and stay in it unless God so clearly directs. My calling is to love them where they are, believing in change but not expecting it.

- **Resist the overwhelm**. Think small and take account of one key relationship in your life. Focus on how you think about that person and your interactions with them, making your intentions and expectations clear all the time. Keep your desires realistic in what an average human being can do. Stick to your own side of the street, meaning you can only change your expectations, not them or their expectations of you, except by answering clearly what you can and cannot fulfill realistically.

- **Put the expectations of others in perspective.** Recognize that what someone else wants from you is their expectation. It does not become yours until you agree to it. If they are a narcissist and focus only on their wants and not yours, you need more help than I can give you in this book.

A great article in determining if someone is a narcissist can be found at www.choosingtherapy. com/married-to-a-narcissist.

- **Stay open to dialoguing** about how you can best meet an expectation someone has for you to strengthen your relationship. Ask yourself if you are fulfilling a reasonable expectation and if not, why not.

- **Maintain perspective**. I don't need to make a big deal about everything that is not going my way in life. Read about a third-world country sometime and see what they are dealing with.

Develop Practical Communication Components

Communication is deceptively simple. We all listen and talk—but the presumption that we do these things effectively is grossly inaccurate. We break away from unhealthy hexpectations by learning and practicing healthy communication skills for self and with others.

- **Honesty.** I must speak truthfully what I think, how I feel, what I need or want. Lying in the moment to pacify a conversation will diminish my integrity and my reputation and break down trust.

- **Understanding**. Seek first to understand where someone else is coming from before working to be understood. Ask open-ended questions like, How does that make you feel? Where do you think that line of thinking will take you? When can we sit down that works for us both? What about this behavior feels like it is helping? You get the picture. Seldom can people answer their why, but good questions can lead to better clarity.

- **Openness**. If you sense a defensive mode in a conversation from yourself or the other party, stop the conversation, because neither is open to really listening for the sake of understanding. You or they just want to deflect and get away from the uncomfortable situation. Step back to the understanding stage and seek clarity and safety before moving forward. Or take a break from the conversation, but ask when it can be discussed safely later without reaction.

- **Validation**. Healthy communication never invalidates another person. Validating someone's feelings makes them feel affirmed, which allows them to feel safe. Restating what you heard from the other person makes them feel listened to and eliminates any misunderstanding in the communicated exchange.

- **Face-to-face communication**. Or ear-to-ear if needed. Many conversations these days are held through messaging, which is tricky. People don't reread it before it's sent (guilty), and body language or tone is assumed. Aura, which is the climate felt, is just as important as the words being said. If we say "I'm not mad" but haven't informed our face, we're giving a double message, and that needs to be addressed.

Develop a Training Mindset

We don't send a Navy SEAL into a hostile territory alone or without proper training, which raises the bar on projected outcomes. A soldier enters boot camp and is trained in hundreds of situations to react a certain way if specific variables happen in the line of duty. Responsible parents train a child to be polite with proper language and manners to be a productive, positive influence in society. Now, if they believe that child will never disobey or react negatively in their life just because they taught their child the right way, it is preposterous. They place a hexpectation on themselves as parents and on the child to act perfectly. We want a soldier and child to ultimately choose to do the right thing because we trained them that way, but there are no guarantees.

Dr. Ashley Smith, author of *The Way I See It: A Psychologist's Guide to a Happier Life,* wrote, "A pessimist dressed in a realist's clothing may say 'expect less to avoid disappointment.' Set that bar low. Things either turn out just the way you expected, or you're pleasantly surprised."

We need to train our minds to think differently. This does not come automatically. Smith continues,

> I agree with "expect less," though in a different way. Expect less. As in expect less frequently. Set fewer expectations period. Don't set the bar lower, but rather, don't set the bar at all. It is the bar itself, not its location, that is the problem. More precisely, it's the mismatch of the bar and reality that robs us of happiness.
>
> So much of what happens around us and to us is, at least in part, out of our direct control. Yet, we strive to control it anyway. These efforts give us the *illusion* of control but really just take time and energy, keeping us from being fully authentic in the moment.
>
> If the mismatch of expectations and reality is what fuels discontent, and we can't actually control (at least some aspects of) reality, why not focus on expectations? Those ARE within our sphere of control. Since we can't always predict or predestine events, trying to match expectations

to the unknown future is a gamble, and I, for one, am not willing to bet my happiness like that. If we let go of expectations (or don't make them in the first place), then we are free to experience things as they happen. While not every moment will be an enjoyable one that we'd like to have continue or repeat, our overall happiness level is less impacted.[35]

Challenge: Practice embracing some uncertainty. Try to enter into some experiences without imagining or planning how it's going to go. Try to catch and erase your expectations about someone else before you interact.

---

35   Ashley Smith, "If You Want to Be Happy, Expect Less," Thrive Global, June 29, 2018, https://community. thriveglobal.com/if-you-want-to-be-happy-expect-less/. Quoted with permission.

CHAPTER FIFTEEN

A FINAL WORD

You must take personal responsibility.
You cannot change the circumstances, the seasons,
or the wind, but you can change yourself.

—JIM ROHN

I'M LEARNING I am enough! Just because I exist, God loves me. In fact, Scripture tells me He rejoices over me with singing (Zephaniah 3:17)—the kind of sound that soothes the soul, not the screeching off-tune kind heard from the driver beside you. It's not based on what I do, how I behave, who I impress, how I dress, or how I speak. He is madly in love with little ole me. This has become my "enough."

That's the beauty of God's grace: "For it is by grace you have been saved, through faith—and this is not from yourselves, it is the gift of God" (Ephesians 2:8–9). Believing I cannot become all things for all people and that all people cannot become all things for me is so freeing!

Learning the art of saying what we want out loud instead of just thinking and hoping people read our minds brings us closer to having our expectations heard and reasonably met. Gaining perspective on what we accept as achievable prevents unrealistic perfectionism from saying nothing is ever good enough.

I hope you better understand how to discern between appropriate and inappropriate expectations. By learning to seek mutual agreement about what is realistically possible in your circumstances and relationships, you can all break free of hexpectations.

"I have changed the dead-end living by opening myself up to endless possibilities and changing my narrative. I'm not hexing my future anymore."—Portia Nelson

CONNECT WITH LYNELLE!

THANK YOU FOR taking the time to read my book! I love connecting with readers and hearing your thoughts, experiences, and questions about what you experienced while reading. Your feedback inspires my writing and helps me grow as an author and coach.

Let's Keep the Conversation Going

Website: Stay updated on my latest projects and Life Discovery journey by visiting my website at hexpectations.com. I am a work in progress out there so keep your expectations in perspective. Grin

ORDER INFORMATION

Additional copies of this book can be ordered
wherever Christian books are sold.